Authentic Amish Cooking

THE Wooden Spoon COOKBOOK

Carlisle Press
WALNUT CREEK

D1019857

Library of Congress Cataloging-in-Publication Data

Miller, Miriam, 1983-
    The wooden spoon cookbook / Miriam Miller
        p. cm.
    Includes index.
    ISBN 1-890050-41-5 (alk. paper)
    1. Cookery, Amish. I. Title

    TX721 .M635 2000
    641.5'66--dc21

                                                            00-050942

The Wooden Spoon Cookbook

© December 2000 Carlisle Press
2673 Township Rd. 421 · Sugarcreek, OH 44681
        First Printing December 2000 5M
        Second Printing July 2001 5M

Pencil drawings by Mary Yoder
Cover photo by Doyle Yoder
Text design by Charity Miller and Virginia Beachy
Cover design by Teresa Hochstetler

ISBN 1-890050-41-5

2673 Township Rd. 421
Sugarcreek, OH 44681

Carlisle Press
WALNUT CREEK

A NOTE FROM MIRIAM

Welcome to the Wooden Spoon Cookbook. I'm happy to share my recipes and life with you in the pages of this book—but first an introduction to my family and myself:

I'm the oldest (I'm 17 now) child in a family of seven. Ivan and Mary are my parents. My dad owns I.M. Painting. My mother takes care of my younger brothers and sisters (and myself!) and our large garden. We all enjoy working together raising corn, beans, peas, carrots, lettuce, and many other garden vegetables.

I have 3 sisters: Sarah (12), Anna (8), and Laura (5) and three brothers: Aaron (16), Marvin (13), and Reuben (9). We have lots of good times together—playing and working!

As you browse through the pages of this book you'll meet more of our family and friends. You'll find it especially delightful to meet my grandparents in my little stories.

Scattered throughout the book you'll meet up with special places and things, like our house that's been home ever since I can remember. And there's the one-room school that holds many fond memories. And my Mom's bell collection, the wishing well in the backyard . . . I'll let you find the rest. They're all mixed in with the recipes in this book, just like Mom's homemade casseroles—a little of this and a little of that. It's all blended together to make a story you'll enjoy.

So pull up a comfortable chair and a cup of coffee or tea and let me tell you a short stories, and when you're ready to make dinner I hope you'll come back. Come back ready to taste Grandma's Bob Andy Pie that she had at her wedding in 1942 (see page 55), Mom's Homemade Bread (see page 4), and my own Soft Batch Cookies (see page 95). I know you'll love it!

Miriam Miller

TABLE OF CONTENTS

Symbols

used in
The Wooden Spoon Cookbook

wooden spoon wisdom

Scattered throughout The Wooden Spoon
are these gems of wisdom about life. I hope
they'll bring a smile to your face, and joy
to the everydayness of cooking.

miriam's memories

In Miriam's memories I'll share a generous slice out
of my life. Childhood memories, a fond recollec-
tion connected to a favorite recipe, and the an-
tics of my parents and siblings are the subjects
of my stories.

Breads and Rolls

Homemade bread
    Is so very good;
I think I'd live on it,
    If I really could.

There's brown bread
    And there's also white,
But the white is
    By far my favorite!

If we buy it out of the store
    We buy the brand called Hillbilly;
But eating store-bought bread
    Makes you feel rather silly!

So let's all just bake
    Our own bread.
"It's also more nutritious!"
    My mother once said!

BREADS AND ROLLS MINI INDEX

wooden spoon wisdom

Gossip is like a balloon; it grows
bigger with every puff.

If you cannot give a good reason for what you are
doing, there is a good reason you should not do it.

Human minds are like wagons.
When they have a light load they are much noisier
than when the load is heavy.

Many things are opened by mistake,
but none so frequently as the mouth.

Half of being smart is knowing what you're dumb at.

The House at the Edge of the Woods

*T*his is our home place, way back on T.R. 654, east of the little town of Mt. Hope, Ohio. Mom's small kitchen garden just made it in the bottom left corner! Our main garden is out of sight behind the house. See the big tank on stilts at the back right corner of the house? That tank contains fuel to heat our house. We also burn wood and coal. Plenty of shade trees and the large woods around the house give us plenty of room to explore and play.

Mom's Homemade Bread
Mrs. Ivan A. Miller
(Miriam's Mother)

1 cup lukewarm water	1 Tbsp. salt
1 Tbsp. brown sugar	1/2 cup shortening
2 Tbsp. yeast	1 qt. warm water
1 cup sugar	flour

In a small bowl, take 1 cup lukewarm water and mix brown sugar and yeast in it. In a large bowl, mix sugar, salt, shortening, and 1 qt. warm water. Add 4 cups flour and beat well. Add yeast mixture. Add 3 more cups of flour and beat well. Keep on adding flour 1 or 2 cups at a time, beating well after each addition. When dough gets too stiff to beat, use your hands to work in enough flour to make a soft dough (greasing hands occasionally). Grease bowl. Turn dough around. Cover; let rise in a warm place. Work down at 45 minute intervals 3 times. Form into loaves. Let rise until double in size. Bake at 350° for 35 minutes.

White Bread
Mrs. Melvin (Esther) Miller

1 cup white sugar	1 cup oil
pinch of salt	flour
2 Tbsp. yeast	

Combine sugar, salt, 2 cups hot water, and 2 cups cold water. Make sure water is warm. Add yeast and let set until yeast dissolves. Add oil and flour to make a nice dough, not too stiff. Let rise; knead and let rise again. Shape into 5 or 6 loaves and put into greased pans. Bake at 350° for 15–20 minutes. Do not overbake. For light wheat bread, add 1 cup of whole wheat flour.

Bread
Mrs. Ammon (Lydia) Miller

about 3 cups flour	1 Tbsp. sugar
1/2 pkg. dry yeast	1 Tbsp. lard
1 tsp. salt	1 cup liquid

This makes 1 loaf of bread.

Brown Bread Recipe *Mrs. Henry (Esther) Miller*

2¼ cups warm water
½ cup sugar
1 cup whole wheat flour
2 Tbsp. yeast
½ cup vegetable oil
1 Tbsp. blackstrap molasses
2 tsp. salt

Mix all together, then let stand for about 5 minutes. Add enough bread flour until right thickness. Knead 15 to 20 minutes, then let rise in Tupperware bowl with lid on. Knead down every 20 minutes for 1 hour. Now put in bread pans and let rise. Bake at 400° till brown, then turn down to 350°. Bake 45 minutes. I also like this dough to make cinnamon rolls.

Banana Nut Bread *Mrs. William (Laura) Miller*

¾ cup sugar
½ cup shortening
2 eggs
2 cups flour
1 tsp. soda
½ tsp. salt
1 cup mashed bananas
1 Tbsp. lemon juice
1 cup chopped nuts

Mix sugar, shortening, and eggs. Sift flour, soda, and salt together. Add sifted dry ingredients to creamed mixture alternately with bananas and lemon juice. Bake in bread pans.

Zucchini Bread

3 eggs
2 cups sugar
3 cups flour
1 tsp. salt
1 tsp. cinnamon
1 cup salad oil
3 cups grated zucchini (unpeeled)
2 tsp. vanilla
1 tsp. soda
1 tsp. baking powder
½ cup coconut
1 cup nuts

Mix all ingredients and bake for 1 hour at 325°, until lightly browned and tests done with a toothpick.

Buns

1½ Tbsp. yeast
1 cup warm water

¼ cup white sugar
1 egg

Beat until foamy.

Add:

2 Tbsp. Lard
3 ½ cups flour

½ tsp. salt

Mix and knead just enough to blend well. Let rise until double in size. Make into buns. Let rise again. Bake at 375° for 15–20 minutes. If all goes well, they can be made in 2 hours.

Biscuit Mix

8 cups flour
⅓ cup baking powder
8 tsp. sugar

2 tsp. cream of tartar
2 tsp. salt

Pack loosely in an airtight container. Method: 1 cup mix to 1 cup milk.

Cinnamon Rolls

1 Tbsp. yeast
¼ cup sugar
3 cups bread flour, divided
1 tsp. salt
2 beaten eggs

¼ cup salad oil
1 cup lukewarm milk
3 Tbsp. melted butter
1 Tbsp. cinnamon
½ cup raisins

Soften yeast in milk; add sugar and 1½ cups flour. When bubbly, add salt, eggs, oil, and 1½ cups flour. Knead; let rise till double in size. Roll to ¼" thick. Spread with melted butter and sprinkle with cinnamon and raisins. Roll like jelly roll and cut into 1½" slices. Place in greased pans. Let rise till double in size. Just before baking, pour a caramelized syrup over it made with ½ cup brown sugar, 1 Tbsp. butter, and ¼ cup water. Bake at 350° for 20 minutes, or until done.

Main Dishes

"What are we having
  For dinner today?"
That's what all of
  My hungry brothers say.

Let's make the casserole
  Called Penny Saver.
With potatoes, hot dogs,
  And peas, oh, what a flavor!

Another day we'll make
  Mashed potatoes and gravy,
Chicken, salad, noodles,
  And green beans it'll be!

At special times it'll be
  Mom's own Pizza Burgers,
A real treat for all
  The big and little workers!

MAIN DISHES MINI INDEX

The Back Porch

*I*t's spring and Mom's morning glories have begun their annual climb from the flowerbed to the back porch eaves.

What a place! The back porch! Large and spacious, it's the perfect place to "eat out" on a warm summer evening. The woods has crept in close enough to provide plenty of shade. My favorite chair, a bowl of popcorn, and a good book—the perfect combination for life without the rest of the world's entertainment.

BBQ Chicken

1 1/2 cups water
1/2 cup vinegar
1/4 oz. Worcestershire sauce
1/2 tsp. pepper

1 oz. garlic powder
1/4 cup salt
1 Tbsp. sugar
1/2 lb. butter or oleo

Spray or brush on chicken every 10 minutes. Keep turning chicken. This is for 5 chickens.

Oven Barbecue Chicken

Using barbecue sauce, dip raw chicken (cut in pieces) into sauce. Place in casserole dish; cover and bake 1 1/2 hours at 325° or until chicken is tender.

Oven Barbequed Chicken

Mrs. Ammon (Lydia) Miller

3 to 4 lbs. chicken pieces
1/3 cup chopped onion
3 Tbsp. butter
3/4 cup ketchup
1/3 c. vinegar
3 Tbsp. brown sugar

1/2 cup water
2 tsp. mustard
1 tsp. Worcestershire sauce
1/4 tsp. salt
1/8 tsp. pepper

Heat oil and fry chicken until brown. Place chicken in a 13x9x2" baking dish. In saucepan, sauté onion till tender. Stir in remaining ingredients. Simmer, uncovered, for 15 minutes. Pour over chicken. Bake at 350° for 1 hour, or until chicken is done.

Baked Chicken

Mrs. John (Marie) Miller

1 cup rice (not minute rice)
1 cup celery
2 tsp. parsley flakes
1/8 tsp. pepper
3/4 cup onions

3 chicken breasts
1/2 tsp salt
1 can cream of mushroom soup
3/4 cup salad dressing
1 1/2 cups water

Put in 12x8" baking dish. Mix cream of mushroom soup, salad dressing, and water; pour over all. Bake at 350° for 1 hour.

Crispy Country Chicken

$^1/_2$ cup Miracle Whip
1 tsp. oregano leaves
1 cup crushed cornflakes
$^1/_4$ cup grated cheese

1 tsp. garlic salt
$^1/_4$ tsp. pepper
1 broiler/fryer chicken, cut up
 (3 to 3 1/2 lbs.)

Mix Miracle Whip and oregano and brush on chicken. Mix cereal, cheese, garlic salt, and pepper. Coat chicken with cereal mixture and place in a 13x9x2" baking dish. Bake at 350° for 1 hour or until baked through.

Chicken or Turkey Bologna

Mrs. Ben Miller

30 lbs. ground meat
10 oz. Tender Quick
1 lb. crackers
4 cups oatmeal

2 cups brown sugar
about 2 Tbsp. black pepper
2 qt. water (approx.)

Mix ground meat and Tender Quick. Let stand overnight, then add rest of ingredients. Can be canned or eaten fresh.

Chicken Bologna
Miss Barbara Miller

25 lbs. raw chicken
1 lb. Tender Quick

Grind twice; let stand for 24 hours.

1 oz. black pepper
$^1/_2$ cup white sugar

2 tsp. saltpeter
$1^3/_4$ Tbsp. liquid smoke

Grind again; mix well. Put in cans. Process as for any other fresh meat.

wooden spoon wisdom

A sharp tongue and a dull mind
are usually found in the same head.

Beef Bologna

Mrs. Aden H. Miller

100 lbs. beef, cut up
27 oz. salt (scant)

32 oz. to 2 lbs. Tender Quick
2 tsp. saltpeter

Sprinkle salt, Tender Quick, and saltpeter over meat and grind. Let set 3 days. Grind again. Mix in the following:

2 oz. black pepper
4 tsp. mace

1 tsp. garlic powder
$1^1/_2$ oz. ground coriander

Add enough water to mix, then mix in with meat. Also mix in 8 quarts of water. Press in jars and add 1 tsp. Liquid Smoke to each quart on top of meat in jars. Cold pack 2 hours. This is also good with turkey or chicken.

Meat Loaf

Mrs. Eli (Verna) Miller

$1^1/_2$ lb. ground beef
$3/_4$ cup crackers
$1/_4$ cup chopped onion
$1^1/_2$ tsp. salt

$1/_4$ tsp. pepper
1 egg, beaten
$3/_4$ cup water

Sauce:

$1/_3$ cup ketchup
2 Tbsp. brown sugar

1 Tbsp. prepared mustard

For meat loaf, combine all ingredients; mix thoroughly. Pack firmly into loaf pan. Combine all ingredients for sauce and pour over meat loaf. Bake at 350° for 1 hour. Let stand 5 minutes before slicing.

Meat Loaf

6 lbs. hamburger
3 cups crackers
1 qt. tomato juice

1 cup onions
8 eggs, beaten
4 Tbsp. salt

Topping:

1 cup brown sugar
1 cup ketchup

$1/_2$ cup mustard

Pour topping over it when it is almost done.

Meat Loaf

4 lbs. hamburger
5 eggs
3/4 cup water
20 crackers
2 slices bread

2 tsp. salt
1/2 tsp. pepper
1 Tbsp. Worcestershire sauce
1/8 cup ketchup
onion

Roast Beef

salt and pepper to taste
unseasoned meat tenderizer
   (1 tsp. per lb. meat)

Mrs. Grass onion soup
   (1 pkg. per 25 lb. meat)

Put salt, pepper, and tenderizer on meat (both sides). Put in Lifetime saucepan. Poke with fork. Pour soup over top; add some water. Bring to boil. Simmer about 4 hours.

Sauce for Baked Hamburger

2 Tbsp. sugar
2 Tbsp. vinegar

2 Tbsp. Worcestershire sauce
1 cup ketchup

Fry hamburger; put in roaster and pour this sauce over it. Bake.

Poor Man's Steak

3 lbs. hamburger
1 cup cracker crumbs
1/2 cup cold water

salt and pepper
1 can cream of mushroom soup

Mix all ingredients well except soup. Make into a roll. Put in refrigerator overnight. Slice and fry. Put in casserole; pour soup over all. Bake at 350° for 1 hour.

Sour Cream Noodle Casserole

Mrs. Jonas (Sadie) Miller

3 - 8 oz. pkgs. noodles
5 lbs. hamburger
1 onion
salt and pepper
3 cans cream of mushroom soup

2 cans cream of chicken soup
16 oz. sour cream
3 cups milk
6 Tbsp. butter
1 lb. Velveeta cheese

Cook noodles in salt water; drain. Fry hamburger and onion together with salt and pepper. Drain off excess fat. Add to noodles. Heat the following in a 4-qt. saucepan on low heat: mushroom soup, chicken soup, sour cream, milk and butter. When hot, add Velveeta cheese and heat till melted. Mix all ingredients together in a large roaster. Bake at 350° until bubbling hot, 1–2 hours.

Chicken Noodle Bake

Combine:

3 Tbsp. margarine, melted
$1/2$ medium onion
1 cup Velveeta cheese
$2^1/2$ cups milk
$1/4$ tsp. pepper

$1/2$ tsp. salt
$1/2$ cup chicken broth
2 cups cream of celery soup
2 cups cooked, deboned chicken

Before baking, add 2 cups uncooked macaroni or 8 oz. noodles. Bake, uncovered, for $1^1/2$ hours at 350°.

Salmon Patties

1 pt. salmon
1 cup bread crumbs
2 eggs
$1/2$ tsp. dry mustard

$1/2$ tsp. paprika
1 sm. diced onion
salt to taste

Combine all ingredients; fry in hot skillet, dropping by spoonfuls in hot grease, turning when brown.

Meat Potato Quiche

3 cups coarsely shredded raw
 potatoes
3 Tbsp. vegetable oil
1 cup grated Swiss or cheddar
 cheese
$1/4$ cup onion (if desired)

$3/4$ cup cooked, diced chicken,
 ham, or sausage
1 cup evaporated milk
2 eggs
$1/2$ tsp. salt
$1/8$ tsp. pepper

Preheat oven to 425°. In a 9" pie pan, stir together potatoes and oil. Press evenly into pie crust shape. Bake for 15 minutes, or until it begins to brown. Remove from oven. Layer next 3 ingredients on hot crust. In a bowl, beat rest of ingredients together. Pour egg mixture onto other ingredients. Return to oven and bake for 30 minutes, or until lightly browned.

Beef or Deer Jerky
Mrs. Paul Hochstetler

meat
salt

Liquid Smoke
black pepper

Cut strips approximately $1/4$" wide from steak (no fat). Shake salt and pepper on each strip and pound thin with meat mallet. Turn each piece and do the same. Brush Liquid Smoke on each side and layer in a pan. Let set till the next morning. Thread a toothpick in the top of each strip and hang on oven rack. Turn oven to 135° and leave oven door open a few inches so moisture can escape. (By using toothpicks you can fill the whole rack and make more at a time.) It usually takes anywhere from 3–5 hours, depending on the thickness of the meat. Check every hour.

Zucchini or Yellow Squash Patties

2 cups squash, peeled and grated
1 tsp. salt
1 Tbsp. sugar

1 egg
$1/2$ cup flour
1 sm. onion, grated

Mix, fry, and eat.

Corned Beef

Mrs. Simon J. Brenneman

50 lbs. beef   3 qt. salt

Place meat in a large crock or similar container and add salt alternately. Let stand overnight, then rinse off roughly and pack in crock again in a brine of:

$^1/_4$ lb. soda   2 lbs. brown sugar
$^1/_4$ lb. saltpeter   2 Tbsp. Liquid Smoke

This meat will be cured and ready to eat in 2 weeks. It can be cut in slices and canned (cold pack 3 hours). Or, if crock is kept in a cool place it can be used up to 3 months.

Mock Ham Loaf
Mrs. Raymond (Anna Mae) Troyer

1 lb. hamburger   1 egg, beaten
$^1/_2$ lb. ground wieners   1 tsp. salt
1 cup cracker crumbs   pinch of pepper

Glaze:

$^3/_4$ cup brown sugar $^1/_2$ tsp. ground mustard
$^1/_2$ cup water   1 Tbsp. vinegar

Mix and add half of glaze with meat mixture, then put in loaf pan. Put remaining glaze over top. Bake at 350° for 1 hour.

Spring Peas and Potatoes

Scrub and peel new potatoes. Cook until tender. Place in bottom of casserole dish. Top potatoes with a thin layer of cooked fresh peas, then cover with a generous amount of white sauce. If desired, sprinkle with cheddar cheese. Since all ingredients are hot, bake just until cheese is melted.

wooden spoon wisdom

The man who says, "What's the use?"
Is never the engine, always the caboose!

Baked Beans

1 can pork and beans	2 diced onions, fried with bacon
1 can kidney beans	1 cup ketchup
1 or 2 cans lima beans	1 Tbsp. mustard
¹/₂ lb. bacon, cut in small pieces	1 cup brown sugar

Do not drain beans. Leave grease on bacon. Mix together and bake uncovered at 350° for 1¹/₂–2 hours.

Wiener Bean Casserole

4 medium potatoes, diced	¹/₄ tsp. black pepper
1¹/₂ cups sweet milk	1 medium onion
³/₄ cup mayonnaise	2 cups cooked or canned
2 Tbsp. flour	green beans, drained
1 tsp. salt	6 wieners, sliced
³/₄ tsp. mustard	

Cook potatoes until tender; drain. Meanwhile, put milk, mayonnaise, flour, salt, mustard, pepper, and onion in blender or whip together. Pour over rest of ingredients; top with bread crumbs. Bake at 350° for 45 minutes. This is a simple recipe that can be made on top of the stove if you're in a hurry.

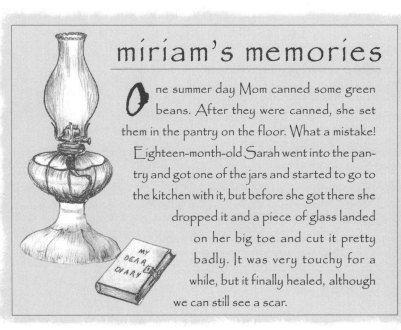

miriam's memories

One summer day Mom canned some green beans. After they were canned, she set them in the pantry on the floor. What a mistake! Eighteen-month-old Sarah went into the pantry and got one of the jars and started to go to the kitchen with it, but before she got there she dropped it and a piece of glass landed on her big toe and cut it pretty badly. It was very touchy for a while, but it finally healed, although we can still see a scar.

Hamburger Vegetable Casserole

1/2 cup diced onion
2 Tbsp. butter
1 lb. hamburger
1 cup diced celery
1 cup sliced carrots
1/3 cup green pepper
1 cube beef bouillon

3/4 cup hot water
1 1/2 tsp. salt
1/8 tsp. black pepper
2 Tbsp. flour
1/4 cup cold water
2 cups mashed potatoes

Sauté onions in butter; add meat and cook until all the pink is gone. Add vegetables, bouillon cube, water, and seasonings. Cover and cook 5 minutes. Mix flour and 1/4 cup water into a smooth paste and add to mixture. Turn into casserole dish. Spoon the mashed potatoes around the edge. Bake at 350° for 45 minutes.

Breakfast Casserole

3 cups cubed bread
3 cups diced ham, sausage, or bacon

3 cups shredded cheese
chopped onion

Grease 7x10" pan. Layer ingredients in order given. Beat 6 eggs; add 1 Tbsp. flour, 2 Tbsp. melted butter, and 3 cups milk. Pour over bread, meat, and cheese. Refrigerate overnight. The next morning, bake uncovered at 325° for 1 hour.

Taco Bake

1 lb. ground beef
1 small onion, chopped
3/4 cup water
1 1/4 pkg. taco seasoning
15 oz. tomato sauce

8 oz. shell macaroni, cooked and
  drained
4 oz. chopped green chilies
2 cups shredded cheddar cheese,
  divided

In skillet, brown hamburger and onion. Drain. Add water, taco seasoning, and tomato sauce. Mix; bring to a boil. Reduce heat and simmer for 20 minutes. Stir in macaroni, chilies, and 1 1/2 cups of cheese. Pour into a greased 1 1/2 qt. baking dish. Sprinkle with remaining cheese. Bake at 350° for 30 minutes or until heated through.

Penny Saver

6 wieners
4 medium potatoes, cooked
1 cup peas
2 Tbsp. minced onion

1/4 cup soft butter
1 Tbsp. mustard
1 can mushroom soup

Mix first 4 ingredients together in casserole. Mix together butter, mustard, and soup; add to potatoes. Dot with wieners. Bake at 350° for 30 minutes.

Chicken Ala King

potatoes, cubed and cooked
noodles, cooked
chicken, cooked and cut up

bread crumbs
chicken gravy

Put in layers by order given in a casserole dish. Bake, uncovered, until top is browned.

Chicken Casserole

chicken
dressing
Velveeta cheese

noodles
gravy

Arrange in a casserole dish or roaster in order given. Bake until hot.

Delicious Hamburger Casserole

1 lb. ground beef, browned
1/2 lb. ground sausage, browned
5 cups bread cubes
5 medium potatoes, cubed and
　　partly boiled
2 eggs

3/4 cup milk
1 small onion, chopped
1/4 tsp. pepper
2 stems of celery, chopped
1 tsp. salt

Mix all ingredients together and put in a baking dish. Cover with 1 can cream of mushroom soup. Bake at 375° for 1 hour, or until done.

Chinese Hamburger Hash

1 lb. ground beef
1 cup chopped celery
2 medium onions, chopped
1 can cream of mushroom soup
1 can cream of chicken soup

$^1/_4$ tsp. pepper
$^3/_4$ cup raw rice
$1^1/_2$ soup cans water
$^1/_4$ cup soy sauce
1 can Chinese noodles

Brown beef; add onions, celery, soup, pepper, water, rice, and soy sauce. Mix well. Place in a greased casserole dish; cover and bake at 350° for 30 minutes. Put noodles on top and bake 15 minutes longer.

Tater-Tot Casserole
Miss Naomi Miller

4 lbs. hamburger, fried with onions
2 bags (frozen) mixed vegetables
2 cans cream of mushroom soup

2 bags (frozen) tater-tots
4 (8 oz.) bags cheddar cheese

Cook vegetables till half tender, then drain water off and cream with soup. Put in a casserole dish in order given. Bake at 300° for $1^1/_2$ hours. (Fills a round Stanley roaster.)

Cheese Soufflé
Mrs. Raymond (Anna Mae) Troyer

8 slices bread
1 lb. cheese, grated
$^1/_4$ cup oleo
sausage, ham, or bacon
2 cups milk

6 eggs, beaten
1 Tbsp. onion salt
salt and pepper to taste
mushrooms (optional)

Cube bread; put in bottom of greased casserole dish. Combine cheese, oleo, and meat. Sprinkle over bread cubes. Mix milk, eggs, and seasonings. Add to top of the other ingredients. Refrigerate overnight. Bake at 325° for 45–60 minutes. Can also add shredded potatoes.

Rice Custard
Mrs. Paul Hochstetler

3 eggs
$^1/_2$ cup brown sugar

2–3 Tbsp. leftover rice
2 cups milk

Mix together. Put in greased casserole dish. Set in larger bowl of hot water and bake at 350° for 2 hours.

My Casserole

Mrs. Alvin (Katie) Brenneman

1½ qt. uncooked wide curly
   noodles, cooked (not too soft)
1 qt. fresh or frozen peas, thawed
1 lb. franks, cut into ¼" slices

4 stems celery, cooked
1 med. onion, chopped and
   cooked

Sauce: Bring to a boil 1 qt. milk. Add a paste of 6 Tbsp. flour with enough milk for consistency. Add 1 lb. Velveeta cheese. Pour over all ingredients and mix. This makes about 5 or 6 qts. Can be made 1 day to bake on the next. Bake at 275° for 1¼ hours. Top with buttered bread crumbs before serving.

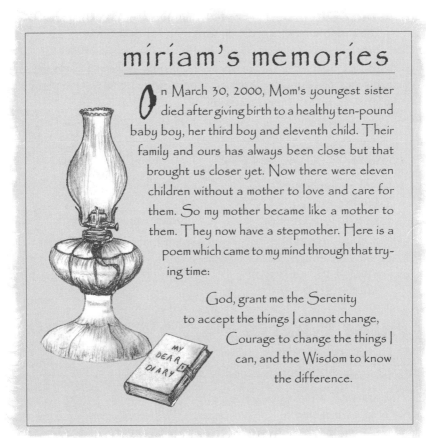

miriam's memories

On March 30, 2000, Mom's youngest sister died after giving birth to a healthy ten-pound baby boy, her third boy and eleventh child. Their family and ours has always been close but that brought us closer yet. Now there were eleven children without a mother to love and care for them. So my mother became like a mother to them. They now have a stepmother. Here is a poem which came to my mind through that trying time:

God, grant me the Serenity
to accept the things I cannot change,
Courage to change the things I
can, and the Wisdom to know
the difference.

Asparagus Casserole

Mrs. Alvin (Katie) Brenneman

5 potatoes
2 onions
2 cups asparagus

$^1/_4$ cup butter
salt and pepper to taste
4 slices cheese

Slice potatoes; put in baking dish. Dice onions and put on top of potatoes. Top with asparagus (fresh or canned). Dot with butter and season. Cover and bake at 325° for 45 minutes. Place cheese on top and melt before serving.

My Pizza Casserole

Mrs. Ivan A. Miller

Cook extra wide noodles in water till tender. Add salt and chicken soup base. Now add pizza sauce (generous amount) and any pizza toppings of your choice (whatever you happen to have on hand—hamburger, sausage, ham, bologna, bacon, peppers, onions, or mushrooms). Mix and pour into casserole dish. Top with cheese. Bake till cheese is melted.

Handy Casserole

Mrs. Wayne Hershberger

6 lg. sliced potatoes
4 cups hamburger
1 can soup (mushroom or celery)

8 cups vegetables (any kind)
salt
Velveeta cheese

Cook potatoes until tender. Brown hamburger. Layer in casserole dish in order given: hamburger, potatoes, soup, cooked vegetables. Cover with cheese. Bake at 350° for 1 hour.

Onion Rings in Batter

large onions
2 egg yolks
$^1/_2$ cup milk

$^3/_4$ cup flour
$^1/_2$ tsp. salt

Cut onions crosswise into $^1/_4$" slices. Separate the slices into rings. Beat egg yolks and add milk. Sift, then stir in flour and salt. Drop the onion rings into batter. Fry them in a kettle of deep fat heated to 395°.

Potluck Potato Casserole

Elsie Miller, Mrs. Ivan A. Miller

2 lbs. boiled potatoes, peeled and chopped
$^1/_2$ stick melted butter
1 tsp. salt
$^1/_4$ tsp. pepper
$^1/_2$ cup chopped onion
1 can cream of chicken soup
1 pt. sweet cream
10 oz. Velveeta cheese
2 cups corn flakes, crushed and mixed with $^1/_4$ cup melted butter

Combine potatoes with $^1/_2$ stick melted butter in a large mixing bowl. Add salt, pepper, onion, soup, sweet cream, and cheese. Blend thoroughly. Pour into greased casserole. Cover with crushed corn flakes mixed with $^1/_4$ cup melted butter.

Chicken Rice Casserole

Mrs. Uriah (Mattie) Weaver

$^3/_4$ cup uncooked rice
1 - 10$^3/_4$ oz. can cream of chicken soup
1 cup water
1 env. onion soup mix
1 fryer chicken (approx. 2$^1/_2$ lb.), cut up (can also use canned chicken)

In a bowl, combine the first 4 ingredients; transfer to greased 1$^1/_2$ qt. baking dish. Arrange the chicken pieces on top. Bake uncovered at 350° for 1$^1/_2$ hours.

Pigs in a Blanket

Slit 8 wieners to within $^1/_2$" of ends and insert 3 thin strips of American cheese. Place each on a crescent roll dough triangle. Wrap dough over wiener and place on ungreased cookie sheet, cheese side up. Bake at 375° for 12–15 minutes or until golden brown.

wooden spoon wisdom

To refuse to admit a mistake
is to make it twice.

Underground Ham Casserole

Mrs. Raymond (Anna) Troyer

4 Tbsp. butter	2 cans cream of mushroom soup
$^1/_2$ cup onion	1 cup milk
1 Tbsp. Worcestershire sauce	4 qt. mashed potatoes
4 cups ham	1 pt. sour cream
2 cups Velveeta cheese	1 lb. bacon, fried and crumbled

Combine first 4 ingredients and cook till onions are tender. Place in bottom of roaster. Heat next three ingredients till cheese is melted. Place on top of first layer. Mash the potatoes, using no salt or milk. Just mix with the sour cream. Spread on top of cheese and soup mixture. Put crumbled bacon on top of all. Bake at 350° for 20 minutes, or until heated through.

One Dish Meal

1 lb. hamburger	diced green peppers
2 cups diced potatoes	1 cup chopped onion
1 cup diced celery	$^1/_2$ cup water
1 cup diced carrots	1 can cream of mushroom soup

Brown hamburger. Combine potatoes, celery, carrots, peppers, and onion. Add water and boil 10 minutes. Add hamburger and place in casserole dish. Add soup. Top with butter and bread crumbs. Bake at 300° for 1 hour.

El Paso Casserole

$1^3/_4$ lb. Velveeta cheese	$1^1/_2$ lbs. noodles, cooked
2 lbs. chipped ham	

White Sauce:

$^1/_2$ lb. white sugar	$^1/_2$ gal. milk
1 cup flour	

Put cheese in the white sauce to melt. Put toasted bread crumbs on top.

Dressing (or Stuffing)

Mrs. Ivan A. Miller

5 eggs
2 cups milk
4 cups toasted bread crumbs
$^1/_2$ cup cubed, cooked potatoes
$^1/_2$ cup diced, cooked carrots
$^1/_2$ cup celery, finely diced
$^1/_2$ cup cooked, diced chicken with
　broth

$^1/_2$ sm. onion, chopped fine
2 tsp. salt
1 tsp. chicken soup base
$^1/_4$ tsp. pepper
parsley

Beat eggs; add milk and bread. Let stand till bread is soaked through. Add vegetables, chicken, onion, and seasonings. Grease a 9x13" loaf pan with butter. Pour the mixture in pan and bake at 375° till set and browned on top. If using canned dressing mix, use 1 qt.

Egg Dutch

5 eggs
1 cup milk
1 Tbsp. flour

salt
pepper

Beat all together with eggbeater. Melt 2 Tbsp. butter in skillet. Pour the mixture in pan and keep on low heat till done. Or, grease a loaf pan with butter. Add mixture and bake at 350° till done.

Breakfast Casserole *Mrs. Ammon (Lydia) Miller*

Beat 6 eggs; add ham, sausage, onion, salt, and pepper to your taste. Pour 2 cups milk and 6 cubed slices of old bread into greased cake pan. Leave in cool place overnight. Bake at 350° for $^1/_2$ hour. Cheese can be put on top, if desired. Very good and tasty.

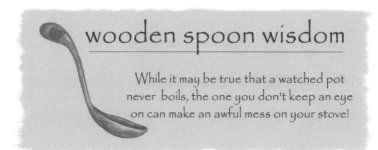

wooden spoon wisdom

While it may be true that a watched pot never boils, the one you don't keep an eye on can make an awful mess on your stove!

Breakfast Casserole

6 beaten eggs
2 cups milk
2 cups bread cubes
1 cup Velveeta cheese, cubed

$^1/_2$ tsp. salt
$^1/_8$ tsp. onion salt (optional)
1 lb. bulk sausage, browned and
chilled

Mix and pour into greased cake pan. Refrigerate overnight. Bake at 350°.
When done, top with Velveeta slices and leave in oven till cheese melts.
Turn several times while baking. Serves 8.

Upside Down Pizza
Mrs. Melvin (Esther) Miller

2 lbs. hamburger
2 cups pizza sauce
pepperoni
green peppers

mushrooms
16 oz. sour cream
mozzarella cheese
2 cans crescent rolls

Brown meat and add salt and pepper to taste. Add pizza sauce. Put into
bottom of casserole dish. Layer with pepperoni, green peppers, and
mushrooms. Bake at 350° for 15–20 minutes. Remove from oven and
cover with sour cream and mozzarella cheese. Top with crescent rolls and
bake until rolls are done.

Popover Pizza

1 qt. hamburger, browned
pizza sauce
diced onion

diced green peppers (if desired)
grated cheese

Mix all together and put in casserole dish. Cover with dough:

2 eggs
1 Tbsp. sugar
1 cup milk

1 Tbsp. vegetable oil
$1^1/_2$ cups Bisquick

Dutch Pizza

Fry potatoes in skillet until tender; add some onions, then a layer of meat
of your choice—you may use several different kinds. Do not stir. Pour raw
scrambled eggs over all. Cover on low heat till done. Melt Velveeta cheese
over it.

Breakfast Eggs

Grease 9x12" pan with 2 Tbsp. margarine. Sprinkle with 1 cup shredded cheese. Put 12 eggs on top of cheese. Poke egg yolks, but don't stir. Sprinkle with salt and pepper. Grate on top 1 can Spam, chipped ham, bacon, or bacon bits. Sprinkle with another cup of cheese. Bake at 350° for 30 minutes.

Sausage Gravy
Mrs. John (Marie) Miller

Brown 1½ lbs. pork sausage in skillet. When done, remove it and melt 1 stick butter; add 2 rounded Tbsp. flour in skillet till bubbly hot. Add milk till it's as thick as you want it. Add sausage and salt and pepper to taste.

Country Chicken and Biscuits

8 slices bacon
2½ cups cubed, cooked chicken
1 - 10 oz. pkg. frozen mixed vegetables, cooked and drained
1 cup chopped tomatoes (about 2 med.)

1½ cups (6 oz.) shredded cheddar cheese
1 can cream of chicken soup
¾ cup milk
1½ cup Bisquick
⅔ cup milk

Put 1 can Durkee french fried onions in greased baking dish. Combine first 4 ingredients and 1 cup cheese. Blend soup and ¾ cup milk. Pour over casserole. Bake covered at 400° for 15 minutes. Meanwhile, combine Bisquick, milk, and ½ cup diced onion; mix thoroughly. Drop by teaspoons to form 6 biscuits around edge of casserole. Bake 15–20 minutes, or until biscuits are golden brown.

Graham Muffins
Mrs. John (Sarah) Brenneman

1 cup whole wheat flour
½ tsp. salt
1 egg
1 tsp. soda
1 cup sour milk

1 cup white flour
1 tsp. baking powder
3 Tbsp. shortening
2 Tbsp. sugar

Drop with spoon into muffin pans. Bake at 425° for 20–25 minutes. Serve with chicken gravy for breakfast.

Featherweight Pancakes

Mrs. Wm. (Laura) Miller

2 cups flour	2 eggs
1 tsp. baking soda	1³/₄ cups sour milk
3 Tbsp. sugar	¹/₄ cup shortening, melted
³/₄ tsp. salt	

Sift together flour, baking soda, sugar, and salt. Combine eggs, milk, and shortening. Add to dry ingredients. Stir only till smooth.

Raw Potato Pancakes
Mrs. Aden H. Miller

6 med. potatoes (raw)	milk to thin
2 beaten eggs	chopped parsley
2 Tbsp. flour	chopped onion
salt	

Peel and grate potatoes and drain in colander; stir in eggs. Add flour and salt to taste; thin with milk for desired thickness of pancakes. Add chopped onion and parsley for added flavor. Fry in medium hot skillet and serve immediately.

Lasagne

1¹/₂–2 lbs. hamburger	1 qt. tomato juice
¹/₂ tsp. garlic salt	1 pkg. spaghetti sauce mix
¹/₂ tsp. seasoned salt	9 strips lasagne noodles

Brown hamburger and add salts. Simmer 10 minutes. Add tomato juice and sauce mix. Simmer 30 minutes. Boil lasagne noodles in salt water with a few drops cooking oil till soft. Put in layers in oblong baking dish: hamburger mixture, noodles, and Velveeta cheese. Makes 3 layers each. Bake at 350° for 20 minutes.

wooden spoon wisdom

He who has a sharp tongue
soon cuts his own throat.

Easy Chicken Potpie
Mrs. Aaron A. Miller

1²/₃ cup frozen mixed vegetables
1 cup diced cooked chicken
1 - 11 oz. can cream of chicken soup

1 cup Bisquick
¹/₂ cup milk
1 egg

Mix vegetables, chicken, and soup in ungreased 9" pie plate. Stir remaining ingredients with fork until blended; pour into pie plate. Bake at 400° for 30 minutes or until golden brown. Serves 6.

Susie's Stromboli
Mrs. Aaron A. Miller

Roll out 1 loaf of homemade or frozen bread dough to about the length of a cookie sheet and about 10" wide. Sprinkle 1 lb. sausage, fried and cooled. Add some pepperoni, onions, ham, mushrooms, peppers, and 1 - 8 oz. package shredded mozzarella cheese. Roll up like jelly roll and pinch edges together. Bake at 350° for ¹/₂ hour.

Potato Puff

3 eggs, separated
¹/₂ cup cream or milk
2 cups mashed potatoes

¹/₄ cup cheese, grated
1 onion, diced

Beat egg whites until stiff. Beat rest of ingredients and fold in egg whites. Pour into greased casserole dish and place in pan of hot water. Bake at 350° for 1 hour, or until puffed or golden brown.

Chicken Supreme
Miss Fannie Miller

2 cups cooked chicken or turkey
2 cans cream of chicken soup
2 cups milk
¹/₂ med. onion, chopped
¹/₂ tsp. salt

¹/₂ tsp. pepper
3 Tbsp. butter
1 cup grated cheese
2 cups uncooked macaroni

Combine all ingredients except macaroni. Add macaroni and refrigerate overnight. Bake at 350° for 1¹/₂ hours. Bake longer for bigger recipes.

Shipwreck

1½ lbs. hamburger, browned
   with onions
1 cup cream of chicken soup
1 cup cream of celery soup

1 pt. carrots, cooked
1 pt. peas, cooked
1 qt. potatoes, cooked and diced

Add cheese and bread crumbs if desired. Season to taste.

Hamburger Grand Style

1½ lbs. hamburger
1 cup chopped onions
1 tsp. salt
8 oz. cream cheese

1 can cream of mushroom soup
¼ cup milk
¼ cup ketchup
2 lbs. tater tots

Brown hamburger and onions. Combine next 5 ingredients and add to
hamburger. Pour into 9x13x2" pan and layer tater tots on top. Bake for ½
hour, or until done.

Mostaccioli

2 lbs. hamburger
2 peppers, diced
2 cups celery, diced
2 cans mushroom soup, diluted
   in milk

1 can tomato soup or juice
¼ lb. Velveeta cheese
1 box mostaccioli
1 lg. onion, diced

Noodles

4 lg. cans College Inn chicken broth
3 qt. water
4 cans cream of chicken soup
pinch of pepper

salt to taste
4 lb. butter
3 heaping Tbsp. chicken base

Put all this in canner and bring to a boil. Add 4 lbs. medium noodles;
bring to a boil again, then let stand 1½ hours. This serves 100 people.

Baked Potato Wedges

potatoes
butter
crushed corn flakes

Wash or peel potatoes; cut into wedges. Dip in melted butter, then roll in corn flakes. Arrange on cookie sheet. Bake at 350° until tender.

Salsa Mac-n-Cheese

1 lb. ground beef
16 oz. chunky salsa
$1^3/_4$ cup water
2 cups elbow macaroni, uncooked
$^3/_4$ lb. (12 oz.) Velveeta cheese

Brown meat in large skillet. Add salsa and water; bring to a boil. Stir in macaroni; reduce heat and cover. Simmer 8–10 minutes, or until macaroni is tender. Add Velveeta; stir until melted.

Pizza Dough

$1^3/_4$ tsp. yeast
$^3/_4$ Tbsp. sugar
1 cup warm water
$2^1/_4$ cups flour
$^3/_4$ tsp. salt
3 Tbsp. oil

Mix yeast, sugar, and water. Add rest of ingredients and mix well. Enough for one pan.

Souper Scalloped Potatoes

$10^1/_2$ oz. cream of mushroom
   or celery soup
$^1/_2$ cup milk
$^1/_2$ cup minced onion
$^1/_2$ tsp. salt
$^1/_4$ tsp. pepper
4 cups sliced raw potatoes
paprika

Combine soup, milk, onion, salt, and pepper. Mix in $1^1/_2$ qt. casserole dish. Cover with $^1/_2$ of the soup mixture. Repeat layers. Bake uncovered at 375° for 1 hour. Uncover and bake 15 minutes longer. Sprinkle with paprika.

Mixed Vegetables

$^1/_4$ cup vegetable oil	1 cup diced potatoes
1 cup stewed tomatoes	1 cup coarsely chopped onions
4 cups cubed summer squash	1 tsp. oregano leaves
$1^1/_2$ cups diced green peppers	$1^1/_2$ tsp. salt
1 cup peas	$^1/_8$ tsp. pepper
1 cup whole kernel corn	1 Tbsp. beef base
1 cup sliced carrots	

Simmer together in 10" skillet for 25–30 minutes. Thicken with $^1/_2$ tsp. cornstarch in 1 Tbsp. water, if desired.

Cornmeal Mush

1 cup cornmeal	3 cups boiling water
1 cup cold water	1 tsp. salt

Grease a 9x5x3" loaf pan. Mix cornmeal and cold water in saucepan. Stir in boiling water and salt. Cook, stirring constantly, until mixture thickens and boils. Cover. Cook over low heat for 10 minutes. Spoon into loaf pan. Cover; refrigerate overnight. Cut into $^1/_2$" slices. Coat slices with flour. Fry in butter on both sides till brown. Makes 9 servings.

Pizza Burgers

Place bun halves, crust side down, on cookie sheet. Spread pizza sauce and pizza toppings of your choice on buns. Top with cheese. Bake at 375° until heated through and cheese is melted.

Onion Patties

$^3/_4$ cup flour	1 Tbsp. sugar
1 Tbsp. cornmeal	1 tsp. salt
2 tsp. baking powder	1 cup diced onions
$^3/_4$ cup milk	

Mix all ingredients together; fry in butter or oil.

Soups

When the soup is simmering,
    Get out your rolling pin.
These crispy, chewy squares are sure
    To make the children grin.

First, you'll need eight cups of flour.
    I like to use whole wheat.
It adds a little texture,
    And makes a healthful treat.

Add two teaspoonfuls of salt,
    And stir the mixture up,
Then a little sweetening—
    A quarter of a cup.

Cut in butter—half a cup,
    Until it looks like meal.
Use your pastry blender with
    An energetic zeal.

Two cups of milk (or even less)
    Are plenty for this dough.
We want to keep it very stiff;
    The reason I will show.

Mix and mix and mix it 'til
    You have to rest your arm.
A little extra kneading
    Won't do it any harm.

Roll it 'til it's very thin,
    Then roll a little longer.
(Now we're glad the dough is stiff—
    It makes it so much stronger.)

Cut it into two-inch squares,
    And roll each square,
And roll each square again.
    (What we're aiming at, you see,
Is dough that's paper thin.)

Bake them at four hundred 'til
    They look like crackers should.
You ought to try this recipe.
    It's really very good.

SOUPS MINI INDEX

wooden spoon wisdom

Worry is like a rocking chair. It keeps
you busy, gets you nowhere.

No man has ever hurt his eyesight
by looking on the bright side of life.

Love is like a butterfly.
It goes wherever it pleases
and pleases wherever it goes.

Happiness is the art of making a bouquet
of those flowers within reach.

One thing about silence is:
No one can go around repeating it.

My One-Room School

Now let's go down the road for a mile or so to West Fairview School. West Fairview Parochial School has been on the small buggy thoroughfare called the Mt. Hope–Winesburg Road since the late 1940s. The Mt. Hope–Winesburg Road connects the mostly Amish village of Mt. Hope to the still smaller village of Winesburg.

I went to school at West Fairview all my life. Well, I should say, all my school life. My brothers and sisters and I go to school only until we're through the eighth grade, like other Amish children.

West Fairview is a one-room school. Well, it's not exactly one room. It has two additional rooms not shown in this picture. One of those rooms says BOYS on the side and the other says GIRLS. There is no running water or heat in these two rooms (some people call them outhouses!). Just the necessities. Nothing more, nothing less.

At West Fairview, I learned to read and write. I also learned other life lessons as well. Playing together, obeying my teacher, and helping my classmates. Yes, I know we weren't perfect (we still aren't!), but I have many fond memories of Fairview School tucked away in the bottom drawer.

Oxtail Soup

1 1/2 lb. lean beef
1 split oxtail
10 cups water
1 tsp. salt
1/4 cup shredded parsley
1/2 c. sliced onion

1/2 cup diced carrots
1 cup diced celery
1 bay leaf
1 Tbsp. quick cooking tapioca
1/2 cup tomato pulp

Cut beef into pieces. Brown oxtail in a little beef fat. Combine the 2 meats. Add water and salt and simmer 4 hours. Add rest of ingredients and simmer 1 hour longer.

Turkey Soup

1 turkey carcass
6 cups water
1 cup carrots
1 cup celery with leaves
1/2 cup turnips
1/2 cup onions

4 cups parsley
1 cup tomatoes
3 Tbsp. barley
1/2 tsp. salt
1/4 tsp. paprika

Cut turkey carcass into pieces and simmer 1 hour. Add water and simmer 1 hour longer. Add rest of ingredients. Serve with crackers.

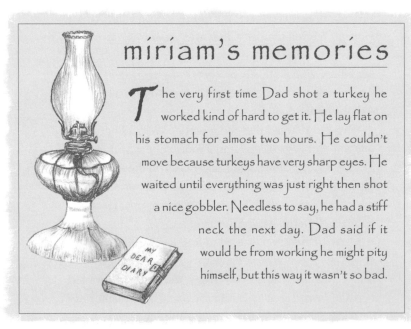

miriam's memories

The very first time Dad shot a turkey he worked kind of hard to get it. He lay flat on his stomach for almost two hours. He couldn't move because turkeys have very sharp eyes. He waited until everything was just right then shot a nice gobbler. Needless to say, he had a stiff neck the next day. Dad said if it would be from working he might pity himself, but this way it wasn't so bad.

Pizza Soup

1 lb. ground beef, browned
  and drained
1 sm. onion, chopped
1 cup sliced mushrooms
1 green pepper, chopped

1 qt. tomato juice
1 cup sliced pepperoni
1 tsp. dried basil
1 tsp. beef base
mozzarella cheese, shredded

In a large saucepan, cook beef, onion, mushrooms, and green pepper. Stir in tomato juice, pepperoni, basil, and beef base. Cook until heated through. Top with cheese. Serve with crackers.

miriam's memories

One Friday in school the boys were stacking wood while the rest of us played Kick the Can. The boys had an assembly line. The first one got a piece of wood and passed it on to the next one and the last one stacked it in a neat row. This seventh grader was supposed to give the wood to Aaron, but one time instead of handing it to him he pitched it. Aaron wasn't looking and the wood hit his head. It started bleeding pretty fast. The teacher got a cold cloth and put it on the cut and it was soon covered with blood. My cousin and I ran home to get my parents. Mom was at Grandpas, so we had to run up there yet. It's a little over a mile from school so we were tired till we got there. By the time we got back home, Aaron, the teacher, and one of the school boys were there. By then his head had stopped bleeding. There was only a tiny spot on his head and we could hardly find it. He was soon on the go and full of pep like always.

Tomato Soup

½ bushel ripe tomatoes
2 bunches celery, chopped
4 lg. onions, chopped
1 cup sugar
1 cup butter
½ tsp. salt
1 tsp. pepper
1 cup clear jel

Boil tomatoes, celery, and onions together for ½ hour. Put through strainer. Bring juice to a boil. Add sugar, butter, salt, and pepper. Mix clear jel with a little water and add. Bring to a boil. Can and seal.

Chunky Beef Soup

1 qt. water
½ can beef soup base mix
1 can (big size) beef broth
2 qt. tomato juice
1 cup white sugar
2 tsp. salt
1 sm. onion, cut fine
2½ lb. hamburger, browned in ½ stick oleo
2 qt. carrots, diced
2 qt. potatoes, cubed
1 qt. peas
1 qt. green beans

Cook vegetables till tender. Thicken with flour paste to the thickness you prefer. Put in jars and cold pack ½ hour. Any vegetables can be used, the kind and amount you want.

Pronto Potato Soup   *Mrs. Uriah (Mattie) Weaver*

8 bacon strips, cut into pieces
  (or any leftover meat)
1 sm. onion, chopped
1½–2 cups leftover mashed potatoes
1 can cream of chicken soup
1 or 2 soup cans milk
2 Tbsp. chopped parsley
salt and pepper to taste
any leftover vegetable can be added

Brown bacon till crisp. Remove; add onions to drippings and sauté 2–3 minutes. Drain off fat. In saucepan, mix potatoes and soup till smooth. Add milk gradually, stirring to avoid lumps. Add bacon, onions, and seasonings. Serve with crackers.

Potato and Ham Soup
Miss Mary Miller

$3/4$ cup butter
$1^1/4$ cup flour
1 small onion, chopped
3 qt. cubed potatoes

3 qt. milk
5 lbs. ham, cubed
$1/2$ box Velveeta cheese
salt and pepper to taste

Put butter in kettle and brown. Add flour to make a paste. Add onion. Put potatoes in another kettle; heat till boiling, then add to browned mixture, water and all. Add milk and ham. Last, add cheese and salt and pepper. Don't boil after adding milk and ham. Serve with crackers. *Delicious.*

Chili Soup

4 onions, chopped
2 lbs. hamburger
2 qt. tomato juice
1 qt. cooked red kidney beans

$3/4$ cup brown sugar
1 - 12 oz. can tomato paste
1 Tbsp. chili powder
salt and pepper to taste

Fry onions in butter. Add hamburger and fry till done. Add the rest of ingredients. Heat and mix well. Put in pressure cooker and process 1 hour at 10 lbs. pressure. 1 batch yields 4 qt.

Bean and Bacon Soup

8 slices bacon, cut in $1^1/2$" pieces
1 lb. navy beans
3 qt. water (if beans are not soaked)
3 cups chopped onions
2 cups diced potatoes
1 cup diced celery

1 cup diced carrots
1 qt. tomato juice
4 tsp. salt
1 tsp. pepper
1 bay leaf

Fry bacon and remove from skillet and add to beans. Cook onions in bacon drippings until soft. Add to beans and bacon, then add rest of ingredients, including bay leaf. Put in jars. Cook 2 hours.

Potato Soup

1 qt. diced potatoes
2 lb. hamburger
2 Tbsp. butter

4 Tbsp. flour
water

Cook potatoes in a large saucepan; fry hamburger in butter. Sprinkle flour over top of meat and mix. Add water to make a gravy. Bring to a boil and add to potatoes. Serve over crackers or bread. Canned hamburger works fine.

Old-Fashioned Bean Soup

1 stick butter
1 cup navy beans, cooked and drained

2 qt. milk
homemade bread (cubed)

Brown butter in saucepan. Add beans and let simmer on low heat a few minutes. Add milk. When hot (not boiling) remove from heat. Add bread till soup is thick enough. Add salt and pepper to taste. If desired, pour brown butter over top.

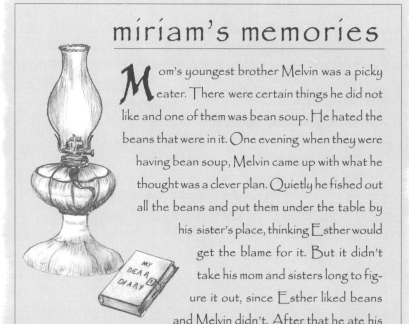

miriam's memories

Mom's youngest brother Melvin was a picky eater. There were certain things he did not like and one of them was bean soup. He hated the beans that were in it. One evening when they were having bean soup, Melvin came up with what he thought was a clever plan. Quietly he fished out all the beans and put them under the table by his sister's place, thinking Esther would get the blame for it. But it didn't take his mom and sisters long to figure it out, since Esther liked beans and Melvin didn't. After that he ate his beans, but he said they tasted like sand with a hard shell around it.

Pies

There's all kinds of fillings
   To put in a pie.
It's hard to decide,
   But I guess I'll try!

Today we'll make
   A fresh peach pie
With a flaky crust
   And the filling piled high.

We'll mix the pie dough
   In a large bowl,
Until it's quite stiff—
   Stiff enough to roll!

Thicken the filling
   And pour it in the crust.
A fresh peach pie
   Is simply a must!

PIES MINI INDEX

The Wood Cookstove

Welcome and come on into our kitchen! Pull up a chair and let me tell you about Mom's cookstove. It's probably the same kind as your grandmother used long ago. We still cook on ours.

On any day, but especially on baking day, we'll load the cookstove with wood and Mom lights it. No knobs. No cords. No bells. No whistles. Baking a cake, for example, at just the right temperature is an art with a woodstove.

Mom and I enjoy our family's cookstove—whether we're making Dad's morning coffee or dinner for company, it serves us well.

Pie Dough

Mix 4 cups flour and 2 Tbsp. brown sugar. Mix in 1 cup lard till crumbly. Beat 1 egg; add a squirt of vinegar and a little water. Mix to crumbs. Enough for 4 pies.

Pie Crust

Mrs. Ammon (Lydia) Miller

3 cups flour
1 cup shortening
1 tsp. salt

2 eggs, beaten
1 tsp. vinegar
water to make $^3/_4$ cup liquid

Fry Pies

Mrs. Ammon (Lydia) Miller

Dough:

$2^1/_4$ qt. Hylite cake flour
1 Tbsp. salt
2 cups water

3 cups Creamtex or Hyscore shortening

Glaze:

2 lb. powdered sugar
$^1/_3$ cup cornstarch
$^1/_4$ cup milk

1 tsp. vanilla
water as needed

Roll out dough very thin. If you don't have a fry pie maker, use the lid of a Lifetime coffee pot for a cutter. Put a spoonful of pie filling on the cut out circles; wet the edges. Fold over to make a half-moon pie. Seal the edges by pressing with a fork. Deep fry in Creamtex or Hyscore shortening. Dip in glaze while pies are still warm. Lay on a rack to dry. (Have your pie filling a little extra thick.)

Coconut Cream Pie

$^1/_2$ cup brown sugar
$^1/_2$ cup white sugar
2 egg yolks
$^1/_2$ tsp. vanilla

$^1/_3$ cup butter
1 Tbsp. flour
1 cup milk
1 cup shredded coconut

Heat milk. Mix sugar, flour, and egg yolks with a little milk. Add to heated milk. Bring to a boil. Remove from heat; add coconut, butter, and vanilla. Pour into a baked pie shell.

Sour Cream Apple Pie

Mrs. Jonas (Sadie) Miller

$^3/_4$ cup white sugar
$^1/_4$ tsp. salt
1 egg
$^1/_2$ tsp. vanilla

2 Tbsp. flour
2 cups chopped apples
1 cup sour cream

Beat egg and add the rest. Bake at 350° for 30 minutes. Top with the following crumbs and bake 15 minutes more.

Crumbs:

$^1/_3$ cup brown sugar
1 tsp. cinnamon

$^1/_2$ cup flour
$^1/_4$ cup oleo

Streusel Apple Pie

$^1/_2$ cup white sugar
3 Tbsp. flour
$^3/_4$ tsp. cinnamon

$^1/_4$ tsp. nutmeg
$^1/_4$ tsp. salt
6 cups sliced apples

Topping:

1 cup rolled oats
$^1/_2$ cup brown sugar
$^1/_2$ tsp. cinnamon

$^1/_2$ cup chopped pecans
$^1/_3$ cup butter, melted

Combine sugar, flour, cinnamon, nutmeg, and salt. Toss apples in sugar mixture. Pour into unbaked pie shell. Combine oats, sugar, cinnamon, nuts, and butter. Sprinkle over filling. Bake at 400° for 40 minutes, or until topping is brown and apples are tender.

Ritz Cracker Pie

Beat 3 egg whites until stiff, adding 1 cup sugar gradually. Fold in 1 tsp. baking powder, 1 cup pecans, and crumbs of 24 Ritz crackers. Add 1 tsp. vanilla. Bake in buttered pan at 350° for 25 minutes. Top with your favorite fruit and whipped topping.

Apple Pie

2 cups raw apples
1 cup sugar
$^1/_2$ cup water

2 Tbsp. tapioca
cinnamon
2 Tbsp. butter

Topping:

1 cup rolled oats
$^1/_3$ cup brown sugar
$^1/_3$ cup nuts

$^1/_3$ cup oleo or butter
$^1/_2$ tsp. cinnamon

Put apples through Salad Master. Mix apples, sugar, water, and tapioca. Put in an unbaked pie shell. Sprinkle with cinnamon and dot with butter. Mix topping ingredients and put on top of apples. Bake at 425°.

Canning Apples for Pie

12 cups sliced apples
5 cups white sugar

6 Tbsp. tapioca
3 cups water

Mix together and cold pack 15 minutes. Don't make jars quite full. Grimes or Golden Delicious are best for this recipe.

No Crust Apple Pie

1 egg
$^1/_2$ cup white sugar
$^1/_2$ cup flour, sifted with baking powder and salt
1 tsp. baking powder

pinch of salt
2 med. apples, peeled, cored, and sliced
$^1/_2$ cup nuts

Beat egg, then add the rest of the ingredients. Mix well and spread in a greased 9" pie plate. Bake at 350° for 30 minutes. Serve warm with ice cream.

wooden spoon wisdom

Catch the bear
before you sell its skin.

Rhubarb Cream Pie

Miss Mary Weaver

3/4 cup rhubarb
3/4 cup sugar
1 cup water
pinch of soda
1 cup milk

1 egg
2 Tbsp. cornstarch
1 Tbsp. butter
1 tsp. vanilla

Boil first 4 ingredients together for 10 minutes. Mix together next 3 ingredients; add to boiled mixture and stir. Bring to a boil. Take off heat and add butter and vanilla.

Rhubarb Delight

1 1/2 cups diced rhubarb
1 cup sugar
1/4 cup water

3 oz. strawberry Jell-O
1 cup Rich's topping
1 tsp. vanilla

Simmer first 3 ingredients together till rhubarb is tender. Stir in Jell-O until dissolved. Cool until partly set. Whip Rich's topping and vanilla. Fold in cream mixture. Pour into baked pie shell.

French Rhubarb Pie

2 cups chopped rhubarb
1 cup sugar
1 egg, beaten

2 Tbsp. flour
1/2 tsp. vanilla

Mix all together and pour in unbaked pie shell. Take 3/4 cup flour, 1/2 cup brown sugar, and 1/3 cup butter; mix into crumbs. Sprinkle on top of pie. Bake in a hot oven until mixture is set and top is browned. Yield: 1 pie.

Rhubarb Pie

Mrs. Paul I. Hochstetler

1 cup chopped rhubarb
1 cup milk
1/2 cup sugar

1 egg yolk
2 1/2 Tbsp. flour

Mix together and put in pie crust and bake. When firm, cover with beaten egg whites and bake again till browned.

Peanut Butter Pie

Crumbs:

$^1/_3$ cup peanut butter   pinch of salt
$^3/_4$ cup powdered sugar

Blend together until mealy. Sprinkle $^1/_3$ of crumbs over pie shell.

Combine:

2 cups milk $^1/_3$ cup flour
$^1/_2$ cup white sugar   3 egg yolks

Heat milk; mix rest of ingredients and mix. Stir into hot milk; bring to a boil. Remove from heat and add 1 Tbsp. butter and 1 tsp. vanilla. Cool; pour into pie shell. Top with beaten egg whites or whipped topping. Sprinkle with the rest of crumbs on top.

Double Peanut Pie

2 eggs $^1/_3$ cup dark corn syrup
$^1/_3$ cup creamy peanut butter   1 tsp. vanilla
$^1/_3$ cup sugar   1 cup salted peanuts
$^1/_3$ cup light corn syrup   1 - 9" unbaked pastry shell
$^1/_3$ cup butter or oleo,   whipped cream or ice cream
   melted

Mix and pour into the crust. Bake at 375° for 30–35 minutes, or until set. Cool; serve with whipped cream or ice cream, if desired.

Peanut Pie

1 cup coarsely chopped salted   3 eggs, beaten
   peanuts   1 tsp. vanilla
$1^1/_2$ cup white corn syrup   1 unbaked pie shell
   (or molasses)

Spread peanuts in the bottom of pie shell. Mix thoroughly: corn syrup, eggs, and vanilla. Pour over peanuts in the pie shell. Add a dash of nutmeg, if desired. Bake at 350° for 45 minutes.

Pecan Pie

¹/₂ cup sugar	1¹/₂ Tbsp. flour
3 eggs, beaten	¹/₂ cup pecans
1 cup light Karo	butter, size of a walnut, melted
³/₄ cup hot water	salt

Mix all ingredients together and pour into unbaked pie shell. Bake at 375° till set.

Surprise Pecan Pie

¹/₄ cup margarine, softened	¹/₄ tsp. salt
1 cup sugar	1 tsp. vanilla
3 eggs	¹/₂ cup chocolate chips
³/₄ cup light corn syrup	¹/₂ cup chopped pecans

Cream margarine and sugar. Add eggs, corn syrup, salt, and vanilla. Stir. Add chips and nuts and stir well. Pour into a 9" pie crust. Bake at 375° for 40–45 minutes. Allow time to set before serving.

miriam's memories

One evening my uncle John came for supper. Mom started fire in the cookstove to make supper. Pretty soon she smelled something burning. She looked around but couldn't see anything. Finally she opened the oven door and all she could see was a heap of tan plastic. She couldn't figure out what it was until she saw a few potato chips and she realized that I had put the chip canister in the oven. I was only a year and a half, so I don't remember it.

Mock Pecan Pie

Mrs. Henry (Esther) Miller

3 eggs, well beaten
$^1/_2$ cup sugar
1 cup dark corn syrup
$^1/_4$ cup butter

$^1/_4$ tsp. salt
$^1/_2$ cup coconut
$^1/_2$ cup quick oatmeal

Mix all together and pour into a 9" unbaked pie shell.

Chocolate Pie

Heat 2 cups of milk.

Mix:

$^3/_4$ cup brown sugar
3 Tbsp. flour

1 Tbsp. cocoa with a little milk

Add to hot milk; bring to a boil. Remove from heat and add 1 Tbsp. butter. Pour into a baked pie shell. Cool; top with whipped cream or topping.

Mock Chocolate Pie

Mrs. Ammon (Lydia) Miller

Heat 1 cup milk and add 22 marshmallows; cool. Beat 1 cup cream and add. Grind chocolate and add. Can also put some chocolate on top. Pour into a baked pie shell. This makes enough for 2 pies.

Butterscotch Pie

Mrs. Aden (Sarah) Miller

Boil till taffy:

2 cups brown sugar
$^1/_2$ cup boiling water
$^1/_2$ tsp. baking soda

butter (size of an egg)
pinch of salt

Mix 6 cups boiling water to boiled mixture. Mix 3 cups sugar, 2 cups flour, and enough water to mix and add. Boil till clear and add vanilla. When cold, pour into 4 baked pie crusts and top with whipped cream.

Butterscotch Pie

1 cup brown sugar   2 Tbsp. milk

Cook 6 minutes.

Add:

1¹/₂ cups rich milk   2 Tbsp. flour
1 egg   1 Tbsp. butter

Put in a baked pie crust and cool.

Lemon Pie   *Mrs. Melvin (Esther) Miller*

3 egg yolks   ¹/₃ cup ReaLemon
1³/₄ cup white sugar   5 cups water
²/₃ cup cornstarch

Mix all ingredients. Cook over low heat until mixture comes to a boil, stirring constantly. Remove from heat and add a chunk of butter. This fills 2 crusts. Top with Rich's topping.

Famous Lemon Pie   *Mrs. Eli (Verna) Miller*

3 Tbsp. cornstarch   3 eggs, separated
1¹/₄ cup sugar   1¹/₂ cup boiling water
¹/₄ cup lemon juice   1 - 9" baked pie shell
1 Tbsp. grated lemon rind ¹/₂ tube soft cream cheese, opt.

Combine cornstarch, sugar, lemon juice, and lemon rind. Beat egg yolks. Add to cornstarch mixture. Gradually add boiling water. Heat to boiling over direct heat, then boil gently for 4 minutes, stirring constantly. After cooled, add cream cheese. Pour into pie shell. Top with Rich's topping.

Cream Cheese Filling for Pie

4 oz. cream cheese   1 Tbsp. sugar
1 Tbsp. milk   1¹/₂ cup Cool Whip

Mix cream cheese, milk, and sugar with wire whisk until well mixed. Gently stir in Cool Whip. Put this in bottom of baked pie shell and top with your favorite fruit.

Pumpkin Pie

3 cups milk
3 eggs, separated
3 Tbsp. flour
1^1/$_2$ cup sugar
1^1/$_2$ cup pumpkin

^{1}/$_4$ tsp. salt
^{1}/$_4$ tsp. cinnamon
^{1}/$_4$ tsp. cloves
^{1}/$_4$ tsp. nutmeg
^{1}/$_4$ tsp. allspice

Heat milk, but do not boil. Beat egg yolks and add flour, sugar, pumpkin, salt, and spices; add this mixture to milk. Last of all fold in beaten egg whites. Mix and pour into two unbaked pie crusts.

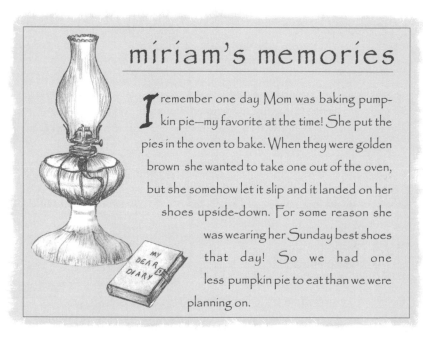

miriam's memories

I remember one day Mom was baking pumpkin pie—my favorite at the time! She put the pies in the oven to bake. When they were golden brown she wanted to take one out of the oven, but she somehow let it slip and it landed on her shoes upside-down. For some reason she was wearing her Sunday best shoes that day! So we had one less pumpkin pie to eat than we were planning on.

Pumpkin Pie

Miss Naomi Miller

3 eggs (save 1 egg white)
^{1}/$_2$ cup white sugar
^{3}/$_4$ cup brown sugar
1 tsp. cinnamon
^{1}/$_8$ tsp. allspice

^{1}/$_8$ tsp. pumpkin pie spice
1 tsp. flour
^{1}/$_8$ tsp. salt
2 Tbsp. pumpkin
2 cups milk, heated

Mix eggs and sugar. Blend well, then add spices, flour, and pumpkin. Add heated milk. Beat egg white and fold in last. More pumpkin can be used if desired. Bake at 425° for 15 minutes, then at 350° for 45 minutes.

Grandpa's Raisin Crumb Pie

Boil:

³/₄ cup raisins	1 Tbsp. vinegar
2 cups water	salt
1 cup brown sugar	

Thicken with 2 Tbsp. cornstarch

Crumbs:

1 cup flour	¹/₂ cup brown sugar
¹/₄ cup shortening	¹/₂ tsp. salt

Raisin Pie Filling

Mrs. Henry (Esther) Miller

1³/₄ qt. water	3 cups (1 lb.) raisins
2 cups sugar	¹/₄ tsp. salt
³/₄ cup clear jel	

Put raisins in large saucepan. Add water, sugar, and salt; boil slowly (covered) for an hour. Mix clear jel with a little water and add. Cornstarch can be substituted for clear jel. Makes enough for 4 large pies.

miriam's memories

Grandma and Grandpa both really like raisin pie. So one day Grandma got a quick notion to make a raisin pie. She was in a hurry to make the filling. After she had the filling made, she set it in the pantry to cool. At suppertime she wanted to pour the filling in the crust and she saw she had forgotten to put the raisins in the raisin pie filling! So she quickly added some raisins. All the grandchildren got a laugh out of Grandma's raisin pie without raisins!

Pineapple Sponge Pie
Miss Esther Weaver

1 cup sugar
3 egg yolks
1 cup milk
1 1/2 Tbsp. flour
1/2 tsp. salt

2 Tbsp. butter
3/4 cup crushed pineapple, drained
3 egg whites, beaten

Mix all together, adding beaten egg whites last. Bake at 425° for 8 minutes, then reduce temperature to 325° and bake 30–35 minutes longer. Makes 1 pie.

Strawberry Pie

5 cans Eagle Brand milk
4 - 1 lb. boxes frozen strawberries, sweetened

2 lg. tubs Cool Whip

Cook Eagle Brand milk in water in can for 1 hour. Stir all together and put in pie crusts. Will make 9 pies. Note: To cook Eagle Brand milk, be sure to remove all labels and keep cans completely covered with water during cooking time. Because of the heat, cans could explode if not covered with water.

Snitz Pie

1 gal. dried apples
10 c. water
4 c. sugar

1 Tbsp. allspice
1 1/2 tsp. cinnamon

Rice Krispie Pie

Beat 2 eggs.

Add:

2/3 cup sugar
1/2 cup Karo
1/4 tsp. salt

3 Tbsp. melted butter
1/2 cup water
1 cup Rice Krispies

Pour in unbaked pie shell. Bake at 400° for 10–15 minutes, then turn back to 300°.

Grape Nut Pie

$^1/_2$ cup Grape Nuts	$^1/_4$ cup butter
$^1/_2$ cup lukewarm water	$^1/_8$ tsp. salt
1 cup brown sugar	3 eggs
1 cup light Karo	1 tsp. vanilla

Soak Grape Nuts in warm water until water is absorbed. Combine sugar, Karo, butter, and salt in saucepan. Quickly bring to a boil and remove from heat. Beat eggs until foamy. Add a small amount of hot syrup mixture to eggs, beating well. Add rest of syrup and mix well. Stir in Grape Nuts and vanilla. Bake in pastry shell at 375° for about 30 minutes. Makes 1 pie.

Grandma's Bob Andy Pie

Mrs. Henry (Esther) Miller
(Miriam's Grandmother)

2 cups sugar	1 tsp. cinnamon
3 Tbsp. flour	3 eggs
$^1/_2$ tsp. cream of tartar	butter size of an egg

Mix dry ingredients; add butter and eggs. Beat; add 3 cups milk. Put in an unbaked pie crust and bake in a hot oven. My Grandma Miller (Esther) served Bob Andy Pie at her wedding in 1942.

Shoo-Fly Pie

Mrs. Henry (Esther) Miller

Mix together till crumbly:

2 cups flour	$^1/_2$ cup shortening
1 $^1/_2$ cups brown sugar	

Take out 2 cups crumbs for top of pie. To remainder of crumbs, add 2 beaten eggs, 2 cups molasses (we use 1$^1/_2$ cups light Karo and $^1/_2$ cup blackstrap molasses), and 1$^1/_2$ cups hot water (not boiling). Mix well. Dissolve 2 tsp. baking soda in $^1/_2$ cup hot water and add. Now put in pie shells and top with crumbs. Bake at 450° for 10 minutes. Reduce heat to 375° and bake 30 minutes, or until top is dry and done. Makes 2 lg. pies.

Vanilla Tart Pie

1 cup sugar
1 cup molasses
1 tsp. vanilla

2 cups water
1 egg

Mix together and pour into 4 unbaked pie crusts.

Topping:

3 cups flour
2 cups sugar
1 egg

1 tsp. baking soda
$^1/_2$ cup lard
1 cup buttermilk

Mix and spoon on top of first part. Bake at 375° till set.

Crumb Pie

1 cup sugar
2 eggs
2 cups molasses

2 Tbsp. flour
4 cups water

Crumbs:

$1^1/_2$ cups flour
$^1/_2$ cup sugar
$^1/_2$ cup lard

1 tsp. cream of tartar
1 tsp. baking soda

Mix first 5 ingredients together; cook well and set aside to cool. Add vanilla. This makes 3 pies.

Dutch Apple Pie   *Miss Ella A. Brenneman*

3 cups sliced apples
1 cup sugar
3 Tbsp. flour
$^1/_2$ tsp. cinnamon
1 beaten egg

1 tsp. vanilla
1 cup light cream
$^1/_2$ cup chopped nuts
1 Tbsp. butter
1 unbaked 9" pie shell

Place apples in pie shell. Mix sugar, flour, and cinnamon. Combine egg, vanilla, and cream; add sugar mixture and mix well. Pour over apples. Sprinkle with nuts and dot with butter. Bake at 350° for 45–50 minutes, till apples are tender.

Cakes and Cookies

'Tis Saturday morn
    And time to bake.
Let's start with cookies
    And end with a cake.

Sometimes to decide
    On what cookies to make
Takes almost as long
    As it does to bake.

Mom wants butterscotch,
    Oatmeal for Sarah, and chips
      for me.
Finally Mom decides
    Chocolate Crinkle it'll be.

Now to make the cake,
    It really isn't hard.
You will be done
    Almost as soon as you start!

CAKES AND COOKIES MINI INDEX

CAKES AND COOKIES MINI INDEX

CAKES AND COOKIES MINI INDEX

Dad's Desk

*N*ow if you'll follow me into the living room, I'll show you my dad's desk.

One of the important things in Dad's desk is the family Bible. You can see it between the two drawers in the middle of the desk. This desk has been in our family for as long as I can remember. And so has the Bible and Dad!

Dad's desk also has a lot of interesting things in it. I remember Dad opening the desk to get money for me to run to the store for Mom.

Almost every Amish home has a desk such as this one. In the top you'll find important books and keep-sakes. In the bottom half, Dad keeps all sorts of things. Maybe you'll have to ask him when he comes in.

My Favorite Chocolate Cake

2 cups white sugar
2 eggs
1 cup sour milk
$^2/_3$ cup cocoa
1 cup shortening
pinch of salt

2 tsp. baking soda
1 tsp. baking powder
1 tsp. vanilla
1 cup brewed coffee
3 cups flour

Put ingredients in bowl in order given. Beat all together for $1^1/_2$ minutes, or 150–200 beats by spoon. Bake at 350° for 30–35 minutes.

Chocolate Cake

Miss Ada P. Hochstetler

$^1/_2$ cup cocoa
2 cups flour
1 tsp. baking soda
2 tsp. baking powder
1 cup white sugar
1 cup brown sugar

2 eggs
$^1/_2$ cup lard
$^1/_2$ cup sour milk or buttermilk
1 tsp. vanilla
1 cup boiling water

Sift cocoa with flour, soda, and baking powder. Mix all together. Add the vanilla and boiling water last. Bake at 350°.

Never Fail Chocolate Cake

$^3/_4$ cup shortening
3 cups brown sugar
3 eggs
$^3/_4$ cup cocoa
$^3/_4$ cup boiling water

$^3/_4$ cup sour milk
3 tsp. baking soda
$1^1/_2$ tsp. vanilla
3 cups flour

Cream shortening and brown sugar; add eggs and mix well. Mix cocoa and water; add to creamed mixture. Add baking soda dissolved in sour milk. Add vanilla and flour. Bake at 350° for 40–45 minutes.

Eggless Chocolate Cake

2 cups brown sugar
$^1/_4$ cup lard
1 cup buttermilk

4 Tbsp. cocoa
$2^1/_2$ cups flour
1 tsp vanilla

Mix all ingredients together. Last of all, add 2 tsp. baking soda dissolved in $^1/_2$ cup boiling water. Bake at 350° for 30 minutes.

Chocolate Chiffon Cake

1/2 cup cocoa
3/4 cup boiling water
1 3/4 cups flour
1 3/4 cups sugar
1 1/2 tsp. baking soda

1 tsp. salt
1/2 cup vegetable oil
7 eggs, separated
2 tsp. vanilla
1/4 tsp. cream of tartar

Icing:

1/3 cup butter or oleo
2 cups powdered sugar
2 oz. unsweetened chocolate,
    melted

1 1/2 tsp. vanilla
3–4 Tbsp. hot water
chopped nuts (optional)

In a bowl, combine cocoa and water until smooth; cool 20 minutes. In a mixing bowl, combine flour, sugar, baking soda, and salt. Add oil, egg yolks, vanilla, and cocoa mixture. Beat until smooth. In another bowl, beat egg whites and cream of tartar until stiff peaks form. Gradually fold in egg yolk mixture. Pour into an ungreased tube pan. Bake at 325° for 60–65 minutes. Invert pan to cool; remove cake from pan.

For icing, melt butter in saucepan. Remove from heat and stir in sugar, chocolate, and vanilla. Stir in enough water to desired consistency; drizzle over cake. Sprinkle with nuts.

Moist Chocolate Cake   *Miss Esther Weaver*

2 cups all-purpose flour
1 tsp. salt
1 tsp. baking powder
2 tsp. baking soda
3/4 cup unsweetened cocoa
2 cups sugar

1 cup vegetable oil
1 cup hot coffee
1 cup milk
2 eggs
1 tsp. vanilla

Sift together dry ingredients in a mixing bowl. Add oil, coffee, and milk; mix well. Add eggs and vanilla; beat 2 minutes (batter will be thin). Pour in large greased cake pan. Bake at 325° for 25–30 minutes.

Coca-Cola Cake

2 sticks margarine
1 cup Coke
2 Tbsp. cocoa
2 cups flour
2 cups sugar

$^1/_2$ cup buttermilk
2 eggs
1 tsp. baking soda
1 tsp. vanilla
$1^1/_2$ cups miniature marshmallows

Heat margarine, Coke, and cocoa to boiling point; pour over flour and sugar. Add buttermilk, eggs, baking soda, and vanilla. Add marshmallows (batter will be thin). Bake in a greased 9x13x2" pan at 350° for 30–35 minutes. Take out when fudgy.

Icing:

$^1/_2$ cup butter
2 Tbsp. cocoa

3 Tbsp. Coke

Heat to boiling and add $^1/_2$ box powdered sugar and 1 cup pecans. Pour over hot cake.

Chocolate Zucchini Sheet Cake

2 cups sugar
1 cup vegetable oil
3 eggs
$2^1/_2$ cups flour
$^1/_4$ cup cocoa
1 tsp. baking soda

$^1/_4$ tsp. baking powder
$^1/_4$ tsp. salt
$^1/_2$ cup milk
2 cups shredded zucchini
1 Tbsp. vanilla

Frosting:

$^1/_2$ cup butter or margarine
$^1/_4$ cup cocoa
6 Tbsp. evaporated milk

4 cups powdered sugar
1 Tbsp. vanilla

In a large mixing bowl, combine sugar and oil. Add eggs, one at a time, beating well after each addition. Combine flour, cocoa, baking soda, baking powder, and salt. Gradually add to the egg mixture alternately with milk. Stir in zucchini and vanilla. Pour into a greased 15x10x1" baking pan. Bake at 375° for 25 minutes. Spread frosting over cake while hot.

Spice Cake

Miss Clara Hershberger

³/₄ cup lard
2 cups brown sugar
2 eggs
2¹/₂ cups flour
2 tsp. baking soda

1 tsp. cinnamon
1 tsp. cloves
1 tsp. nutmeg
1 cup buttermilk

Combine lard and brown sugar; add eggs. Sift together flour, baking soda, cinnamon, cloves, and nutmeg. Add dry ingredients alternately with buttermilk. Bake at 350° for 30 minutes.

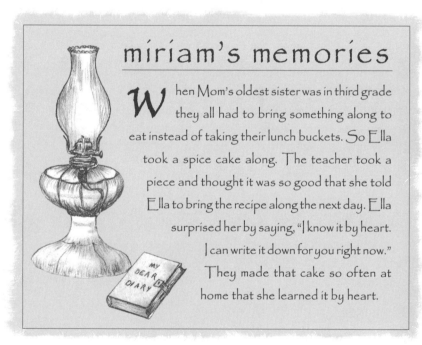

miriam's memories

When Mom's oldest sister was in third grade they all had to bring something along to eat instead of taking their lunch buckets. So Ella took a spice cake along. The teacher took a piece and thought it was so good that she told Ella to bring the recipe along the next day. Ella surprised her by saying, "I know it by heart. I can write it down for you right now." They made that cake so often at home that she learned it by heart.

Banana Orange Bars

2 cups mashed bananas
  (3–4 bananas)
1 cup vegetable oil
2 tsp. cinnamon
1 tsp. baking soda

1²/₃ cups sugar
4 eggs
2 cups flour
2 tsp. baking powder
1 tsp. salt

Bake in a 15x10x1" pan. Frost with Orange Butter Frosting. Yield: 3 dozen.

Marble Cake

Light Part:

1/2 cup butter	2 cups flour
1 cup white sugar	2 tsp. baking powder
1/2 cup sweet milk	4 beaten egg whites
1 tsp. vanilla	

Dark Part:

1/2 cup butter	1 tsp. nutmeg
1 cup brown sugar	1 tsp. cloves
4 egg yolks	1 tsp. cinnamon
1/2 cup sour milk	1 tsp. baking soda
1 1/2 cups flour	

Light Part: Cream butter and sugar. Add milk and vanilla. Beat well and add flour and baking powder. Mix in beaten egg whites.

Dark Part: Cream butter and sugar. Add egg yolks and mix well. Mix in sour milk. Add flour, nutmeg, cloves, cinnamon, and soda. Put this batter by spoonfuls and same amount of Light Part batter alternately into greased pan. Bake at 350° for 45 minutes.

Nutmeg Cake

1/2 cup butter	1 tsp. baking soda
1 1/3 cups sugar	1/2 tsp. salt
3 eggs	1 tsp. baking powder
2 cups sifted flour	1 cup buttermilk
2 tsp. nutmeg	

Topping:

6 Tbsp. butter	1 cup brown sugar
1/4 cup light cream	1/2 cup flake coconut

Cream butter and sugar till light; add eggs, one at a time, beating well after each addition. Add dry ingredients alternately with buttermilk, beating until smooth. Bake at 375° for 20 minutes.

For topping, cook butter, cream, and brown sugar to boiling. Remove cake from oven. Pour hot mixture slowly over cake. Sprinkle with coconut. Return to oven; bake 5 minutes longer.

Caramel Cake

Mrs. Eli (Verna) Miller

Cream together:
2 cups brown sugar $^1/_2$ cup lard

Next, add:
2 eggs (unbeaten)   2 cups all-purpose flour
1 tsp. vanilla

Put 1 tsp. cocoa in a cup. Add 2 tsp. hot water. Fill the cup with sour milk, then add 1 tsp. baking soda. Stir this mixture until cocoa is well dissolved. The cup will run over, so be sure to hold it over the mixing bowl while stirring. When cocoa is dissolved, pour in with the other ingredients and mix. Bake at 350°.

Turtle Cake

Miss Susie M. Miller

1 chocolate cake mix or your   1 stick butter
    favorite recipe   1 can Eagle Brand milk
1 bag caramel candy

Bake $^1/_2$ of the cake batter in sheet pan. Melt caramel candy; add butter and Eagle Brand milk. Mix and put on top of baked cake. Pour on remaining batter and top with chocolate chips and nuts. Bake at 350° until top is done.

Coffee Cake

$^1/_3$ cup shortening   1$^1/_2$ tsp. baking powder
$^3/_4$ cup sugar $^1/_4$ tsp. salt
1 egg   1 Tbsp. vinegar (fill with milk
2 tsp. vanilla   to make 1 cup liquid)
2 cups flour   1 tsp. baking soda

Beat shortening and sugar; add egg and vanilla. Mix dry ingredients alternately with vinegar, milk, and baking soda. Sprinkle with brown sugar and cinnamon and $^1/_2$ cup melted margarine. Bake in a 13x9x2" pan at 400° for 20 minutes.

Cream Filled Coffee Cake

Scald 1 cup milk.

Add:

1 stick margarine	1 tsp. salt
$^1/_2$ cup sugar	

Beat 2 eggs in a large bowl and add milk mixture. Dissolve 1 pkg. yeast in $^1/_4$ cup warm water and add. Mix in $3^1/_2$ cups flour and let rise. Put in 3 - 9" pans. Spread crumbs on top; let rise. Bake at 350°

Crumbs:

$^1/_4$ cup margarine	$^1/_2$ cup brown sugar
$^1/_2$ cup flour	

Cream Filling:

$1^1/_2$ cups milk	6 Tbsp. flour

Cook and cool.

Stir in:

$1^1/_2$ cups Crisco	$1^1/_2$ cups powdered sugar
vanilla	salt

Cut cakes in half and spread cream filling between halves.

Sour Cream Coffee Cake

Mrs. John (Marie) Miller

$^1/_2$ cup walnuts, finely chopped	8 oz. sour cream
1 tsp. ground cinnamon	1 tsp. baking powder
$^1/_2$ cup sugar	1 tsp. baking soda
$^1/_2$ cup softened margarine or butter	1 tsp. vanilla
1 cup sugar	2 large eggs
2 cups flour	

In small bowl, combine nuts, cinnamon, and $^1/_2$ cup sugar. Set aside. Grease 9" pan or tube pan with removable side. Beat butter with 1 cup sugar until light and fluffy. Add flour and rest of ingredients. Beat until blended, constantly scraping sides of bowl with spatula. Spread half of batter in pan; sprinkle half of nut mixture on top. Spread evenly with remaining batter. Top with rest of nut mixture. Bake at 350° for 60–65 minutes, until cake pulls away from pan.

Variation—Apple Sour Cream Coffee Cake: Slice 1 med. size cooking apple thinly with $^1/_2$ of nut mixture in middle of batter. Top with remaining batter and nut mixture.

Cherry Coffee Cake

1 loaf bread dough
21 oz. cherry pie filling
$^1/_2$ cup butter or margarine
$1^1/_4$ cups flour
$1^1/_4$ cups sugar

Spread bread dough in 15x10x1" baking pan. Spread with pie filling. In a bowl, mix butter, flour, and sugar until crumbly; sprinkle over filling. Bake at 375° for 25–30 minutes.

Fruit-Filled Coffee Cake

Mrs. John (Sarah) Brenneman

3 eggs
$1^1/_2$ cups sugar
$^3/_4$ cup oil
1 tsp. vanilla
3 tsp. baking powder
3 cups flour
juice of 1 orange (or water and
    orange flavor)

Pour half of batter in pan. Spread with 1 can fruit pie filling. Add rest of batter. Sprinkle with sugar and cinnamon. Bake at 350° for 15 minutes. Reduce temperature to 320° and bake 1 hour longer.

Walnut Wonder Cake

4 cups flour
2 tsp. baking powder
1 tsp. soda
$^1/_2$ tsp. salt
1 cup butter or oleo
2 cups sugar
2 cups milk

Topping:

$^2/_3$ cup brown sugar
2 tsp. cinnamon
1 cup chopped walnuts

Pour half of batter in pan and sprinkle with half of topping and rest of batter and crumbs on top. Bake at 350°. Drizzle or frost with caramel frosting.

Walnut Graham Torte

1 cup butter or margarine
1 cup sugar
3 eggs, lightly beaten
2 cups graham cracker crumbs
$^1/_2$ cup flour
1 tsp. baking powder
$^1/_2$ tsp. cinnamon
$^1/_4$ tsp. salt
1 cup milk
2 cups diced, peeled apples
1 cup chopped walnuts
$1^1/_2$ cups whipped cream
3 Tbsp. powdered sugar

In a large mixing bowl, cream the butter and sugar. Add eggs; mix well. Combine graham cracker crumbs, flour, baking powder, cinnamon, and salt; add to creamed mixture alternately with milk and mix well. Fold in apples and $^3/_4$ cup walnuts. Spread into 3 greased 8" round cake pans. Bake at 350° for 25–30 minutes. Whip cream and powdered sugar until stiff; spread between layers and on top of torte. Sprinkle with remaining walnuts.

White Hickory Cake

3 cups flour
3 tsp. baking powder
2 cups sugar
$^1/_2$ cup butter
1 cup sweet milk
1 cup nuts

Combine flour and baking powder. Beat sugar and butter until creamy. Alternately add flour mixture and milk to batter. Add nuts. Bake at 350° for 30 minutes.

Apple Walnut Cake

Mrs. Allen (Edna) Brenneman

3 eggs, beaten
2 cups sugar
$^1/_2$ cup vegetable oil
2 tsp. vanilla
2 cups all-purpose flour
2 tsp. baking soda
2 tsp. ground cinnamon
$^1/_2$ tsp. ground nutmeg
$^1/_4$ tsp. salt
4 cups diced, unpeeled apples
1 cup coarsely chopped walnuts

In a large mixing bowl, beat together eggs, sugar, oil, and vanilla. Combine flour, baking soda, cinnamon, nutmeg, and salt; mix into batter. Fold in apples and nuts. Spread into 13x9x2" baking pan. Bake at 325° for 50–60 minutes, or until cake tests done; cool. Frost. Yield: 12–15 servings.

Apple Cake

2 eggs
1 1/2 cups white sugar
1/2 cup margarine
1 tsp. cinnamon
1 tsp. nutmeg

1 tsp. baking powder
1 tsp. baking soda
1/2 tsp. salt
1 1/2 cups flour
3 1/2 cups shredded apples

Topping:

1/2 cup margarine
1/2 cup brown sugar
1/2 cup cream or 1/4 cup milk

1 rounded Tbsp. flour
1/2 cup white sugar

Mix in order given. Bake at 350° for 40–45 minutes. Put topping on cake while both are warm.

For topping, mix together and cook until well blended and starting to thicken.

Harvest Time Crumb Cake

6 apples, cubed
3 cups flour
1/2 tsp. salt
1 1/2 cups sugar
1 1/2 cups milk

4 tsp. baking powder
2/3 cup butter
3 eggs, beaten
1 tsp. vanilla
a few drops of lemon juice

Crumbs:

1 cup butter
1 cup brown sugar
1 cup white sugar

1 1/2 cups flour
2 tsp. cinnamon
1/4 tsp. nutmeg

Cube enough apples for about 6 cups or more, if desired. Toss in a bit of sugar and lemon juice. Proceed with batter as for any cake, using the next eight ingredients. Grease a baking dish and spread batter in pan and top with apples. Sprinkle crumbs on top and bake at 350° for 45 minutes.

Old-Fashioned Fresh Apple Cake

1 cup salad oil
2 eggs
2 cups sugar
2¹/₂ cups flour
1 tsp. baking soda
1 tsp. salt

1 tsp. cinnamon
1 tsp. baking powder
1 cup pecans or black walnuts
3 cups chopped apples
6 oz. butterscotch chips

Mix well. Spread mixture in greased 13x9x2" pan. Distribute butterscotch chips on top of cake. Bake at 350° for 55–60 minutes. Cool and cut into squares. For best results, bake 1 day before serving.

Butterscotch Brownies

¹/₄ cup butter
1 cup brown sugar
1 egg
1 cup flour

1 tsp. vanilla
¹/₂ tsp. salt
1 tsp. baking powder
¹/₂ cup chopped nuts

Mix together and pour in loaf pan. Sprinkle sugar over top. Bake at 350° for 30 minutes. Cut in squares while hot.

Apple Dapple Cake   Mrs. Ivan A. Miller

3 eggs
2 cups sugar
1¹/₂ cups salad oil
3 cups flour
1 tsp. baking soda

1 tsp. salt
2 tsp. vanilla
1¹/₂ cups chopped nuts
3 cups chopped apples

Bake in greased 8x9" tube pan at 350° for 1 hour. While cake is still hot, glaze can be put over it.

wooden spoon wisdom

Grudges, like babies,
grow larger when we nurse them.

Oatmeal Apple Crumb Cake

1 1/2 cups white sugar
1 cup brown sugar
3 cups quick oats

4 cups flour
1 1/2 cups shortening
pinch of salt

Mix all ingredients together. Keep 2 cups of crumbs to put on top. Dissolve 2 rounded tsp. baking soda in 3 cups buttermilk. Pour this into the crumbs; add 2 tsp. cinnamon, 1 tsp. nutmeg, 1 tsp. cloves, 3 cups finely chopped apples, and 2 beaten eggs. Mix, but don't stir hard. Top with the 2 cups reserved crumbs. Bake in 9x13x2" pan at 350° for 1 hour.

Fiesta Banana Cake

1/2 cup shortening
1 1/3 cups sugar
2 cups flour
1 tsp. baking powder
1/2 tsp. baking soda
1/2 cup sour milk or buttermilk, divided

1 cup mashed ripe bananas
2 eggs (unbeaten)
1 tsp. vanilla
1/2 cup chopped nuts

Stir shortening to soften; add dry ingredients. Add 1/4 cup milk and mashed bananas. Mix until flour is dampened. Add eggs, vanilla, nuts, and remaining milk. Beat 1 minute. Pour into greased pan and bake at 350° for 35–40 minutes.

Blue Ribbon Banana Cake

3/4 cup butter or oleo, softened
1 1/2 cups sugar
2 eggs
1 cup mashed ripe bananas
2 cups flour, sifted
1 tsp. baking soda

1/2 tsp. salt
1/2 cup buttermilk
1 tsp. vanilla
1/2 cup chopped pecans
1/2 cup coconut

In a large mixing bowl, cream butter and sugar until fluffy. Add eggs; beat 2 minutes. Add bananas; beat 2 additional minutes. Set aside. Sift together flour, soda, and salt; add to creamed mixture alternately with buttermilk and vanilla. Beat well; stir in nuts. Turn into 2 lightly greased 9" round cake pans. Sprinkle half of the coconut on batter. Bake at 350° for 25–30 minutes. Remove cake from pan and cool. Spread creamy nut filling on one layer. Place remaining cake layer, with coconut side, on top of filling. Frost with creamy white frosting.

Orange Cake

Mrs. Eli (Verna) Miller

2³/₄ cups cake flour
1¹/₂ cups sugar
1¹/₂ tsp. soda
³/₄ tsp. salt
1¹/₂ cups buttermilk
¹/₂ cup butter or margarine

¹/₄ cup shortening
3 eggs
1¹/₂ tsp. vanilla
1 cup golden raisins, chopped
¹/₂ cup finely chopped nuts
1 Tbsp. grated orange peel

Grease and flour baking pan. Measure all ingredients into large mixing bowl and stir well. Bake at 350°.

Williamsburg Butter Frosting:

¹/₃ cup butter or margarine
3 cups confectioner's sugar

3–4 Tbsp. orange juice
2 tsp. grated orange peel

Fruit Cocktail Cake

1¹/₂ cups sugar
2 cups flour
2 eggs
1 tsp. vanilla

2 Tbsp. lemon juice
2 tsp. baking soda
³/₄ tsp. salt
16 oz. fruit cocktail (with syrup)

Pour in a 13x9x2" pan and sprinkle with topping ingredients. Bake at 350° for 35–40 minutes.

Meanwhile, combine all sauce ingredients in a medium saucepan and bring to a boil. When cake is done and still warm, pour sauce over cake.

Topping:

¹/₂ cup packed brown sugar

¹/₂ cup coconut

Sauce:

¹/₄ cup evaporated milk
³/₄ cup sugar
1 tsp. vanilla

¹/₂ cup butter or margarine
¹/₂ cup coconut
¹/₂ cup walnuts

wooden spoon wisdom

Friendship is a lighted candle
Which shines most brightly
When all else is dark.

CAKES AND COOKIES

Pineapple Dump Cake

2 cups flour
$^1/_2$ tsp. salt
$1^1/_2$ cups white sugar

2 tsp. soda
1 tsp. vanilla
2 cups crushed pineapple

Dump all ingredients in a bowl and mix well. Bake at 350° for 35 minutes in an ungreased 9x13x2" pan.

Black Bottom Banana Bars

$^1/_2$ cup softened butter or margarine
1 cup sugar
1 egg
1 tsp. vanilla
$1^1/_2$ cups mashed ripe bananas
  (about 3 med.)

$1^1/_2$ cups flour
1 tsp. baking powder
1 tsp. baking soda
$^1/_2$ tsp. salt
$^1/_4$ cup cocoa

Mix well, then divide batter in half. Add cocoa to half; spread into a greased 13x9x2" baking pan. Spoon remaining batter on top and swirl with a knife. Bake at 350° for 25 minutes.

Delicious Oatmeal Cake

$1^1/_4$ cups boiling water
1 cup oatmeal
1 stick margarine
1 cup brown sugar
1 cup white sugar
2 eggs, beaten

$1^1/_3$ cups flour
1 tsp. baking soda
1 tsp. baking powder
1 tsp. cinnamon
1 tsp. salt

Pour boiling water over oatmeal and margarine. Cool 15 minutes. Add rest of ingredients and bake at 350° for 45 minutes.

Topping:

1 cup brown sugar
4 tsp. margarine

$^1/_2$ cup cream or milk
1 cup coconut

Mix milk, margarine, and sugar and bring to a boil. Add coconut and pour over hot cake. Return to oven for 10 more minutes.

Shoo-Fly Cake

4 cups flour
³/₄ cup shortening
2 cups brown sugar

2 cups boiling water
1 cup molasses
1 Tbsp. baking soda

For crumbs, mix flour, shortening, and brown sugar. Set 1 cup of crumbs aside for topping. To the rest of the crumbs, add the water, molasses, and baking soda; mix well and pour into greased cake pan. Sprinkle with reserved crumbs. Bake at 350°.

Jell-O Cake

Bake yellow cake mix. Let cool 15 minutes, then poke holes in cake with meat fork. While cake is cooling, make Jell-O as directed on package. Pour Jell-O slowly and evenly over cake. Refrigerate. Prepare 1 large pkg. vanilla (or whatever flavor you prefer) instant pudding according to directions. Spread on top of cake. Spread 1 small container of Cool Whip on top. Decorate with nuts, coconut, etc.

Angel Food Cake

Step 1: Measure and sift together 3 times:
1 cup flour   ⁷/₈ cup sugar (³/₄ cup + 2 Tbsp.)

Step 2: Measure in a large mixing bowl:
1¹/₂ cups egg whites   1¹/₂ tsp. vanilla
1¹/₂ tsp. cream of tartar   1¹/₂ tsp. salt

Beat with wire whisk until foamy; gradually add ³/₄ cup sugar, 2 Tbsp. at a time. Beat about 10 seconds after each addition, until meringue is firm and holds stiff peaks.

Step 3: Place flour and sugar mixture in sifter and sift about 3 Tbsp. over the surface of meringue. Fold gently with rubber scraper until flour/sugar mixture disappears, turning bowl a quarter turn each stroke. Bake in a 9" tube pan.

Lightning Cake

2 eggs
butter the size of an egg
1 tsp. vanilla
milk

1 cup flour
1 cup sugar
1 heaping tsp. baking powder

Put eggs, butter, and vanilla in a measuring cup. Fill with milk to one cup. Put in bowl and add dry ingredients; beat well. Bake in 8x8" pan at 350°.

German Crumb Cake

Sift:

1 cup sugar
2 cups flour
$^1/_2$ tsp. salt

1 tsp. cinnamon
1 tsp. nutmeg
1 tsp. cloves

Mix with:

$^1/_2$ cup butter
1 egg
2 Tbsp. molasses

1 cup sour milk
1 tsp. soda

Remove half of the crumbs and save for topping. Mix last 4 ingredients with remaining crumbs. Pour into greased pan and top with remaining crumbs. Bake at 350° for 45 minutes.

Cinnamon Cake

Cake:

1 cup sugar
1 tsp. cinnamon
2 Tbsp. butter
1 cup milk

$^1/_2$ tsp. salt
2 tsp. baking powder
2 cups flour

Syrup:

$1^1/_2$ cups water
$1^1/_2$ cups brown sugar

1 Tbsp. butter

Mix cake and pour into 13x9x2" pan. Heat water, brown sugar, and butter; pour over batter. Bake at 350° for 30–40 minutes. Good with ice cream.

Butterscotch Cake

4 Tbsp. vinegar
2 tsp. vanilla
1 cup white sugar
1 cup brown sugar
2 cups flour

$^1/_4$ cup cocoa
$^1/_2$ cup lard or butter
1 tsp. baking soda
$^1/_4$ tsp. salt
2 eggs

Put vinegar and vanilla in a cup and fill up with water. Put all in bowl and beat. Bake in loaf or layer pans at 350°.

Coffee Cake

$1^1/_4$ cup sugar
1 cup vegetable oil (scant)
1 cup butter or buttermilk
1 tsp. vanilla

2 cups flour
1 tsp. baking powder
$^1/_2$ tsp. soda
$^1/_2$ tsp. salt

Pour half of batter into greased 13x9x2" pan. Stir together $^1/_4$ cup brown sugar and 1 Tbsp. cinnamon. Sprinkle half of this mixture on batter. Pour on rest of batter. Sprinkle on remaining cinnamon and sugar. Bake at 350° for 30 minutes. Poke holes in hot cake with fork.

Beat together and make a thin glaze:

1 cup powdered sugar
$^1/_2$ tsp. vanilla

hot water

Pour over cake.

Fluffy White Cake

2 cups sugar
$^1/_2$ cup shortening
1 cup lukewarm water
$2^1/_2$ cups flour

4 tsp. baking powder
1 tsp. vanilla
4 egg whites, beaten

Mix together, adding beaten egg whites last. Pour into a greased 13x9x2" pan. Bake at 350°.

Jelly Roll

4 eggs, separated
3/4 cup white sugar
3/4 cup bread flour

1 tsp. baking powder
1/4 tsp. salt
1 tsp. vanilla

Filling:

6 level Tbsp. flour
1 cup hot water

3/4 cup brown sugar

Beat egg yolks well; add sugar, flour, baking powder, salt, and vanilla. Last add well-beaten egg whites. Bake at 400° for 13 minutes.

For filling, combine ingredients and heat till thick, stirring constantly. Remove from heat and add 1 Tbsp. of butter, vanilla, or maple flavoring.

Do Nothing Cake

2 eggs
2 cups sugar
2 cups flour
1 tsp. baking soda

1 tsp. vanilla
1 - #2 can crushed pineapple,
    drained

Topping:

1 stick margarine
1 cup sugar
2/3 cup milk

1 cup chopped nuts
1 cup coconut

Mix by stirring lightly. Pour into greased 13x9x2" pan. Bake at 350° for 25–30 minutes. Boil topping ingredients together for 5 minutes. Put on top of cake while still warm.

Carrot Cake

2 cups flour
1 tsp. baking soda
1/2 tsp. salt
1/2 tsp. nutmeg
1 tsp. allspice
1 tsp. cinnamon
3 Tbsp. lemon juice

1/2 cup shortening
1/4 cup sugar
3/4 cup honey
2 beaten eggs
1 cup grated carrots
1 cup raisins
1 cup rolled oats

In a bowl, sift dry ingredients. Add rest of ingredients to dry mixture. Pour into greased pan. Bake at 325° for 50 minutes or until done.

Healthy Carrot Cake
Miss Ada P. Hochstetler

1 1/2 cups fructose
3/4 cup melted oleo
4 eggs
2 cups flour
2 tsp. soda

1 tsp. baking powder
2 tsp. cinnamon
1 tsp. salt
3 cups raw carrots, grated
1 cup nuts

Cream fructose and oleo; add eggs. Beat well. Sift flour, soda, baking powder, cinnamon, and salt. Add to creamed mixture and fold in carrots and nuts.

Fudge Nut Bars

2 cups shortening
4 cups brown sugar
4 eggs
4 tsp. vanilla

4 cups flour
2 tsp. baking soda
2 tsp. salt
6 cups quick oats

Fudge Nut Filling:

1 can Eagle Brand milk
1 pkg. chocolate chips
2 Tbsp. oleo

1/2 tsp. salt
1 cup nuts
2 tsp. vanilla

Mix dough and spread a thin layer in 2 cookie sheets. For filling, put milk, chips, oleo, and salt in saucepan. Put on low heat. Mix till melted and smooth. Stir in nuts and vanilla; spread over dough. Dot remainder of oatmeal mixture over chocolate filling. Bake at 350° for 25–30 minutes.

Chocolate Chip Blonde Brownies

2/3 cup soft butter
2 cups brown sugar
2 Tbsp. hot water
2 eggs
2 tsp. vanilla

2 cups flour
1 tsp. baking powder
1/4 tsp. soda
1 tsp. salt
1/2 cup chocolate chips

Cream butter and sugar; add hot water, eggs, and vanilla. Beat well. Add dry ingredients. Spread in greased 13x9x2" pan. Sprinkle chocolate chips over top. Bake at 350° for 25–30 minutes. Cool slightly and cut into squares.

Chocolate Mint Brownies

1 cup all-purpose flour
1/2 cup softened butter or margarine
1/2 tsp. salt
4 eggs

1 tsp. vanilla extract
16 oz. chocolate flavored syrup
1 cup sugar

Filling:

2 cups confectioner's sugar
1/2 cup softened butter or margarine
1 Tbsp. water

1/2 tsp. mint extract
3 drops green food coloring

Topping:

1 - 10 oz. pkg. mint chocolate chips   9 Tbsp. butter or margarine

Combine the first 7 ingredients in a large mixing bowl; beat at medium speed for 3 minutes. Pour batter into a greased 13x9x2" baking pan. Bake at 350° for 30 minutes (top of brownies will still appear wet). Cool completely.

Combine filling ingredients in a medium mixing bowl; beat until creamy. Spread over cooled brownies. Refrigerate until set.

For topping, melt chocolate chips and butter over low heat in a small saucepan.

Double Chocolate Bars

1/2 cup oleo
3/4 cup white sugar
2 eggs
1 tsp. vanilla
1/4 tsp. baking powder

3/4 cup flour
1/2 cup nuts
2 Tbsp. cocoa
1/4 tsp. salt
2 cups marshmallows

Cream oleo and sugar. Beat in eggs and vanilla. Add dry ingredients and nuts. Spread in bottom of small jelly roll pan. Bake at 350° for 15–20 minutes. Remove from oven and sprinkle marshmallows evenly on top. Return to oven for 2 more minutes. Cool, then top with the following.

In saucepan, melt together 6 oz. chocolate chips and 1 cup peanut butter. Add 1 1/2 cups Rice Krispies. Spread on bars. Chill and cut into squares.

Chocolate Chip Bars

Miss Sarah Miller

4 eggs
2 cups brown sugar
1 stick oleo

2 cups flour
2 tsp. baking powder
1 cup chocolate chips

Mix first 5 ingredients and pour into a greased cookie pan. Sprinkle chocolate chips on top. Bake at 350° for 25 minutes.

Chocolate Peanut Butter Bars

$^1/_4$ cup vegetable oil
$^1/_2$ cup sugar
$^1/_3$ cup brown sugar
$^1/_2$ cup peanut butter
1 egg
2 Tbsp. water
1 tsp. vanilla

$1^1/_4$ cups flour
$^3/_4$ tsp. baking soda
$^1/_2$ tsp. baking powder
$^1/_4$ tsp. salt
$^3/_4$ cup chocolate chips
$^1/_2$ cup chopped walnuts

Pour into ungreased 13x9x2" pan. Bake at 350° for 20 minutes. Remove from oven and sprinkle with $^1/_4$ cup chocolate chips. Let chips melt and spread as frosting. Sprinkle with nuts, if desired. Cut into bars.

Peanut Butter Bars

Mrs. Jr. (Naomi) Miller

1 cup oleo
1 cup brown sugar
1 cup sugar
2 eggs
1 tsp. soda

$^1/_2$ tsp. salt
1 tsp. vanilla
2 cups flour
2 cups oats

Mix and press into large cookie sheet and bake at 350° for 25 minutes, or till done. Sprinkle with chocolate chips while cake is still hot.

Mix 1 cup powdered sugar, $^1/_2$ cup peanut butter, and 8 or more Tbsp. milk to glaze consistency. Drizzle this over top and swirl slightly with knife. Cut into bars while warm.

The Park

Out behind the house, in the woods, our family built park. Now understand when I say 'built' it means that Dad built the playhouse, Mom built the path, and my little brothers built the campfire.

Many a summer night we roast hot dogs and marshmallows. We enjoy our "park", humble though it may be. It's better than all the vacations and sightseeing trips in the world. It's where memories are made.

Peanut Butter Fingers

Mrs. Henry (Esther) Miller

2 cups brown sugar
2 eggs
1 cup shortening
2^1/$_2$ cups flour
2^1/$_2$ cups oatmeal

^{2}/$_3$ cup peanuts
^{1}/$_3$ cup water
1 tsp. soda
^{1}/$_2$ tsp. salt
1 tsp. vanilla

Spread on large cookie sheet and bake. Cool partly before glazing.

Glaze:

3 Tbsp. water

2 Tbsp. butter

Bring to a full boil. Remove from heat and add 1 cup powdered sugar and vanilla. You may need more powdered sugar. ^{1}/$_4$ cup cocoa may also be added. Beat until smooth, then spread and cut into bars.

Peanut Butter Bars *Mrs. Uriah (Mattie) Weaver*

16 eggs
3 qts. brown sugar
2^2/$_3$ cups shortening
1 qt. peanut butter
3 Tbsp. vanilla

2 tsp. salt
2 qts. coconut
2^2/$_3$ Tbsp. baking powder
2^1/$_2$ qts. flour

Mix all together. Spread ^{1}/$_2$" thick on cookie sheets and bake at 350° for 20 minutes. When cool, cut in bars. Makes approximately 175 bars.

Pumpkin Dessert Squares

1 box yellow cake mix
^{1}/$_2$ cup butter, melted
3 eggs
3 cups pumpkin pie mix

^{2}/$_3$ cup milk
^{1}/$_4$ cup sugar
1 tsp. cinnamon
^{1}/$_4$ cup butter

Reserve 1 cup dry cake mix. Combine remaining mix with melted butter and 1 egg. Spread in bottom of jelly roll pan. Mix together pumpkin pie mix, remaining eggs, and milk; pour over top. Combine reserved cake mix, sugar, cinnamon, and butter until crumbly and sprinkle over top. Bake at 350° for 40–45 minutes.

Peanut Butter Bars

Mrs. Ella A. Brenneman

$^1/_2$ cup softened butter or margarine
$^1/_2$ cup sugar
$^1/_2$ cup brown sugar
$^1/_2$ cup creamy peanut butter
1 egg, beaten
1 tsp. vanilla extract

1 cup all-purpose flour
$^1/_2$ cup quick cooking oats
1 tsp. baking soda
$^1/_4$ tsp. salt
1 cup (6 oz.) semi-sweet
   chocolate chips

In a mixing bowl, cream butter, sugars, and peanut butter. Add egg and vanilla; mix well. Combine flour, oats, baking soda, and salt; stir into the creamed mixture. Spread into a greased 13x9x2" baking pan. Sprinkle with chocolate chips. Bake at 350° for 20–25 minutes. Combine icing ingredients; drizzle over bars.

Icing:
$^1/_2$ cup powdered sugar
2 Tbsp. creamy peanut butter

2 Tbsp. milk

Frosted Pumpkin Bars

Verna P. Hochstetler, Mary Miller

4 eggs, beaten
1 cup oil
1 cup pumpkin
2 cups sugar
$^1/_2$ tsp. salt

1 tsp. baking soda
1 tsp. baking powder
2 tsp. cinnamon
2 cups flour

Frosting:
3 oz. cream cheese
6 Tbsp. butter, melted
$2^1/_2$ cups powdered sugar

1 tsp. vanilla
1 tsp. milk

Mix together and bake at 350° for 20 minutes in floured cookie sheet.

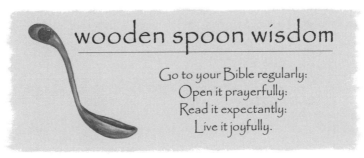

wooden spoon wisdom

Go to your Bible regularly:
Open it prayerfully:
Read it expectantly:
Live it joyfully.

Pumpkin Bars

Miss Wilma Miller

2 cups brown sugar
2 eggs, beaten
1/2 cup oil
1 cup pumpkin
1 cup nuts

2 cups flour
1/2 tsp. salt
2 tsp. cinnamon
1 tsp. soda
1 tsp. baking powder

Frosting:

3 1/2 cups powdered sugar
3 oz. cream cheese
6 Tbsp. melted butter

1 tsp. vanilla
milk

Fruit Bars

1/2 lb. margarine
1 cup sugar
1 tsp. vanilla

2 eggs
2 cups flour
1 cup nuts (optional)

Beat margarine and sugar; add eggs and beat again. Add rest of ingredients and mix until well blended. Spread 2/3 of dough onto greased 13x9x2" pan, then spread 1 can cherry or pineapple pie filling on top. Put remaining dough over pie filling in small blobs scattered around. Bake 40–45 minutes at 350°. Sprinkle powdered sugar over top after baking.

Fruit and Nut Bars

1 cup white sugar
1 cup brown sugar
1 cup butter or margarine
3 eggs
1 cup nuts
4 Tbsp. milk

4 cups flour
1 tsp. cinnamon
1 tsp. nutmeg
1 tsp. baking soda
1 cup dates

Spread on cookie sheet and bake at 350° for about 12 minutes. Sprinkle with powdered sugar and cut into squares when almost cool.

Caramel Apple Bars

Crust:

1/2 cup butter or margarine	1 cup rolled oats
1/4 cup shortening	1 tsp. salt
1 cup packed brown sugar	1/2 tsp. baking soda
1 3/4 cups flour	1/2 cup chopped pecans

Filling:

4 1/2 cups coarsely chopped, peeled apples	14 oz. caramels
3 Tbsp. flour	3 Tbsp. butter or margarine

In a mixing bowl, cream butter, shortening, and brown sugar until fluffy. Add flour, oats, salt, and soda; mix well. Stir in pecans; set aside 2 cups. Press remaining oat mixture into the bottom of an ungreased 13x9x2" baking pan.

For filling, toss apples with flour; spoon over crust. In a saucepan, melt the caramels and butter over low heat; drizzle over apples. Top with the reserved oat mixture. Bake at 400° for 25–30 minutes. Cool before cutting into bars.

Apple Danish

Pastry:

3 cups flour	1/2 tsp. salt
1 cup shortening	1 egg yolk
1/2 cup milk	

Combine and make like pie dough.

Filling:

6 cups sliced apples	1 1/2 cups sugar
2 Tbsp. flour	1 Tbsp. cinnamon

Glaze:

1 egg white, lightly beaten	1/2 cup powdered sugar
2–3 Tbsp. water	

Bake at 375° for 40 minutes; cool. Drizzle with glaze.

Fruit Cake Bars

1 cup brown sugar
1¼ cups water
⅓ cup shortening
2 cups raisins
2 cups flour
1 tsp. salt

2 tsp. cinnamon
1 tsp. baking soda
1 tsp. baking powder
½ tsp. nutmeg
1 tsp. cloves

Combine first 4 ingredients in a saucepan and bring to a boil. Remove from heat and cool. Blend in rest of ingredients. Spread in greased 13x9x2" pan. Bake at 350° for 30–40 minutes. Cool and cut into bars.

Raisin Bars

1 cup water
Boil 5 minutes; cool.

1 cup raisins

Add:
   ½ tsp. soda

   ½ tsp. salt

Cream:
   ½ cup shortening

   1 cup sugar

Add:
   1 egg
   Mix with raisin mixture.

   1 tsp. vanilla

Sift:
   2 cups flour
   1 tsp. soda

   1 tsp. cinnamon

Add to creamed mixture. Add ½ cup nuts. Bake in a jelly roll pan at 350°.

Glaze: Blend powdered sugar and milk; drizzle over warm bars. When cool, cut into squares.

wooden spoon wisdom

Worry is interest on trouble
before it comes due.

Sour Cream Raisin Bars
Miss Lydia Troyer

1³/₄ cups oatmeal	1 tsp. baking soda
1³/₄ cups flour	1 tsp. baking powder
1 cup sugar (brown and white)	salt
1 cup oleo	vanilla

Filling:

4 egg yolks	2 cups sour cream
1 cup white sugar	2 cups raisins
1 Tbsp. cornstarch	

Pat ²/₃ of crumbs in pan. Bake 15 minutes; cool. Put all of filling together and boil. Stir often (it burns easily). Pour over crumbs and cover with remaining crumbs. Bake 20 minutes.

miriam's memories

We have a small playhouse that Mom and Dad gave us for Christmas one year. One day Reuben climbed up on the playhouse roof. Aaron saw him and told him to come off. He said, "I'll just jump off. I've jumped higher than this already!" He wanted to jump and somehow lost his balance and fell, hitting his head on a rock, which cut a gash in his forehead. He started for the house, leaving a trail of blood behind him. One of the children saw it and ran into the house for Mom. Mom came running and tried to stop the bleeding, but it took a while. After the bleeding had stopped, Dad came home from painting and they took him to the doctor for a few stitches. As far as I know, he never jumped off the playhouse again.

Cowboy Bars

2 cups brown sugar
2 cups white sugar
2 cups margarine
4 eggs, beaten
2 tsp. vanilla
1/2 cup milk

4 cups flour
3 tsp. baking powder
pinch of salt
3 cups oatmeal
1 1/2 cups coconut
2 cups chocolate chips

Combine all ingredients and mix well. Place in 2 jelly roll pans. Spread evenly and press lightly. Bake at 350° for 20–30 minutes.

Coconut Love Bars

1 cup flour
3 Tbsp. brown sugar
1 stick butter
1 1/2 cups coconut

1 1/2 cups brown sugar
4 Tbsp. flour
2 eggs, beaten
1 tsp. vanilla

Mix first 4 ingredients and pat evenly in greased 7x15" pan. Bake at 325° for 10 minutes. Mix rest of ingredients and pour over baked crumbs. Bake 30 minutes or more. Cool and cut into squares.

Yum Yum Bars

Miss Mary P. Hochstetler

4 eggs
2 cups brown sugar
1 stick oleo
2 tsp. baking powder

2 cups flour
2/3 cup raisins
2/3 cup chopped nuts

Mix together. Bake on cookie sheet at 350° for 25 minutes. Cut into bars and remove from cookie sheet while hot. Chocolate chips or coconut can be used instead of raisins and nuts, if desired.

Coffee Bars

2 2/3 cups brown sugar
1 cup vegetable oil
1 cup warm coffee
1 tsp. salt
1 tsp. vanilla

2 eggs
1 tsp. soda
1 cup nuts
3 cups flour

Put everything in bowl and beat well. Top with 1 cup chocolate chips. Bake at 350° for 25–30 minutes.

Squares

1²/₃ cups graham cracker crumbs
¹/₂ cup flour
¹/₂ cup brown sugar
1 Tbsp. water

1 cup chopped nuts
¹/₂ tsp. baking soda
¹/₂ cup melted margarine
2 cups chocolate chips

Combine cracker crumbs, flour, and soda; set aside. Mix margarine, sugar, eggs, water, and vanilla. Gradually add flour mixture; mix well. Stir in 1 cup chips and nuts. Spread in greased 11x7x2" pan. Bake at 375° for 18 minutes, or until lightly browned. Remove from oven. Immediately sprinkle 1 cup chips over warm surface. Let stand until chips soften. Spread evenly. Cool and cut into squares.

Delicious Brownies

2 cups sugar
¹/₄ cup cocoa
1 cup melted butter
4 eggs
2 tsp. vanilla

1¹/₂ cups flour
1 tsp. salt
1 tsp. baking soda
¹/₂ cup walnuts, chopped

Mix sugar, cocoa, and butter; add eggs and vanilla. Sift flour, salt, and baking soda and add to creamed mixture. Fold in walnuts. Pour into greased jelly roll pan. Bake at 350° for 25 minutes. Cool and frost.

Cream Cheese Brownies   Mrs. Aaron A. Miller

1 cake mix
8 oz. cream cheese
1 egg

¹/₂ cup sugar
1¹/₂ cups chocolate chips

Mix chocolate cake mix as directed on box. Pour into 13x18" pan. Beat together cream cheese, egg, and sugar. Drop onto cake batter with spoon, then swirl with knife. Sprinkle with chocolate chips. Bake at 350° for 30 minutes, or until done.

wooden spoon wisdom

A smile is a curve
that helps set things straight.

Gumdrop Bars

Mrs. Wayne Hershberger

2 cups sifted flour
$^1/_4$ tsp. salt
1 tsp. cinnamon
3 eggs
2 cups brown sugar

$^1/_4$ cup evaporated milk
1 cup soft gumdrops, cut into
   small pieces
$^1/_2$ cup chopped nutmeats

Sift flour, salt, and cinnamon together. Beat eggs until light and beat in sugar and milk gradually. Add flour mixture gradually. Add gumdrops and nuts. Spread in greased pan and bake at 325° for 25 minutes. Cut into bars and roll in powdered sugar. Makes 40 bars.

miriam's memories

One winter day while the rest of the children were in school, Anna and Laura went to Grandpa's house for a while. Suddenly Laura came running and said Dad has to come and help Anna. We quickly went, not knowing what to expect. We didn't have to go far before we could hear her crying. We have a string beside the path through the woods to hold on to when it's slippery. Well, she was sliding her hand over it as she walked and somehow got her finger tangled in it. She couldn't get loose, so she had to stand there and wait till Dad came to free her.

Yum Yum Cookies

Mrs. Aden H. Miller

2 cups flour
$^1/_2$ cup brown sugar

$^1/_2$ cup butter

Mix thoroughly and press firmly in bottom of large cookie sheet.

Mix together:

3 eggs
2 cups brown sugar
$^1/_2$ tsp. salt
1 cup coconut

$^1/_2$ cup chopped nuts
2 Tbsp. flour
$^1/_4$ tsp. baking powder
1 tsp. vanilla

Spread over first mixture in cookie sheet. Bake at 350° for 20 minutes, or until brown. Cut into bars when cool.

Monster Cookies

$1^1/_2$ sticks oleo
1 cup white sugar
1 cup brown sugar
4 eggs
1 lb. chunky peanut butter

$2^1/_2$ tsp. soda
4 cups oatmeal
$^1/_2$ lb. M&Ms
12 oz. chocolate chips

Add more oatmeal, if necessary, to make a stiff dough. Form teaspoon size balls and roll in powdered sugar. Bake at 350° for 10 minutes. Do not overbake.

wooden spoon wisdom

Quarrels never could last long
If on one side were all the wrong.

Apple Pastry Squares

Filling:

1/4 cup packed brown sugar

2 Tbsp. cornstarch

1 cup water

5 cups thinly sliced peeled apples

1/2 tsp. cinnamon

1/4 tsp. nutmeg

1 Tbsp. lemon juice

Pastry:

2 cups flour

1/2 tsp. salt

2/3 cup shortening

2 egg yolks, beaten

1/4 cup cold water

1 Tbsp. lemon juice

Glaze:

1/2 cup powdered sugar

1 Tbsp. milk

1 Tbsp. butter or oleo

1/2 tsp. vanilla

For filling, combine sugar, cornstarch, and water in a saucepan. Mix until well blended. Add apples; heat to boiling, stirring constantly. Reduce heat and simmer 5 minutes, stirring occasionally. Remove from heat and stir in spices and lemon juice. For pastry, mix like pie dough. Roll out to fit the bottom and halfway up the sides of a 13x9x2" baking pan. Spread filling over pastry. Roll remaining pastry to fit pan exactly; place on top of filling. Fold bottom pastry over top and press to seal. Cut a few small slits on top crust. Bake at 400° for 40 minutes, or until lightly browned. For glaze, combine all ingredients and drizzle over warm pastry.

Marble Squares

Mrs. Ivan A. Miller

2 1/2 cups brown sugar

2 1/2 cups white sugar

2 1/2 cups margarine

2 1/2 tsp. salt

6 eggs

3 tsp. vanilla

7 3/4 cups flour

1 tsp. baking soda

2 tsp. baking powder

1 1/2 cups nuts

1 1/2 cups chocolate chips

Cream sugar, oleo, eggs, and vanilla; add flour, soda, baking powder, and salt. Spread in 2 jelly roll pans. Sprinkle chips on top. Put in oven for 1 minute. Take out and marbleize with knife. Sprinkle nuts on top. Bake at 350° for 20 minutes.

Chocolate Snowcaps

$^1/_2$ cup softened margarine
$1^2/_3$ cups sugar
2 eggs
$^1/_2$ tsp. vanilla
2 cups flour

$^1/_2$ cup cocoa
1 tsp. baking powder
$^1/_2$ tsp. salt
$^1/_3$ cup milk

Chill dough 2–3 hours. Form into 1" balls; roll in powdered sugar. Bake on lightly greased baking sheets at 350° for 10–12 minutes.

Soft Batch Cookies
Miriam Miller

1 cup white sugar
1 cup brown sugar
$^1/_2$ cup oleo
2 eggs

3 cups flour (no more)
$1^1/_2$ tsp. baking soda
1 tsp. salt
2 cups chocolate chips

The dough will be very dry, but if too dry, add a very small amount of water. Bake at 350°.

Peanut Chocolate Chip Cookies

2 cups flour
2 tsp. baking powder
$^1/_2$ tsp. salt
1 cup margarine
1 cup sugar
1 cup brown sugar

2 eggs
1 tsp. vanilla
1 cup creamy peanut butter
1 cup Spanish peanuts
1 cup chocolate chips

Combine dry ingredients; set aside. Cream shortening and sugar; add eggs and vanilla and beat until fluffy. Blend in peanut butter. Gradually add dry ingredients. Stir in peanuts and chocolate chips. Drop by teaspoonfuls onto cookie sheet. Bake at 350° for about 8 minutes.

Chocolate Chip Cookies

²/₃ cup butter or oleo
1 cup white sugar
1 cup brown sugar
2 eggs
2 tsp. vanilla

3¹/₄ cups flour
1 tsp. soda
1 tsp. salt
6 oz. chocolate chips
³/₄ cup nuts

Drop by teaspoonfuls onto ungreased cookie sheet. Bake at 375° for 8–10 minutes.

Chocolate Krispie Cookies

4 eggs
2 cups oleo, softened
4 cups sugar
4 tsp. vanilla
8 cups Rice Krispies

1 tsp. salt
5 cups flour
2 tsp. soda
24 oz. chocolate chips or M&Ms

Mix together and drop on greased baking sheet. Bake at 350° about 10 minutes or until lightly browned.

Chocolate Chip Cookies

2 cups brown sugar
1 cup white sugar
2 tsp. salt
2 cups shortening
1 tsp. vanilla

4 tsp. soda
6 eggs
4 tsp. cream of tartar
7 cups flour
2 or 3 pkg. chocolate chips

Drop by teaspoonfuls onto cookie sheet. Bake at 375°. Nuts may be added, if desired.

wooden spoon wisdom

Love never asks how much must I do,
but how much can I do.

Bakeless Chocolate Cookies

$1/2$ cup sugar
2 Tbsp. butter
$1/4$ cup milk

$1^1/2$ cups rolled oats
3 Tbsp. cocoa
vanilla

Boil sugar, butter, and milk together for 3 minutes. Remove from heat and add the rest of ingredients. Mix thoroughly and drop by teaspoonfuls onto cookie sheet. When cold, roll in powdered sugar.

No-Bake Cookies

2 cups white sugar
3 Tbsp. cocoa
$1/4$ cup butter
$1/2$ cup milk

3 cups rolled oats
$1/2$ cup peanut butter
1 tsp. vanilla

In saucepan, mix first 4 ingredients. Bring to a boil and boil 1 minute. Remove from heat and add the rest. Mix well. Drop quickly by teaspoonfuls onto waxed paper.

Chocolate Crinkle Cookies

2 cups sugar
$3/4$ cup vegetable oil
$3/4$ cup cocoa
4 eggs
2 tsp. vanilla

$2^1/3$ cups flour
2 tsp. baking powder
$1/2$ tsp. salt
powdered sugar

Mix well. Cover and chill. Bake at 350° for 12 minutes. Roll in powdered sugar before baking.

Chocolate Nut Drop Cookies

1 cup white sugar
4 Tbsp. butter
1 egg
$1/2$ cup milk

$1^1/2$ cups flour
$1/2$ cup cocoa
2 tsp. baking powder
1 cup chopped nuts

Drop on well-buttered cookie sheet. Bake at 375° for 15 minutes.

Oreo Cookies

Mrs. Raymond (Anna) Troyer

1 - 18 oz. cake mix (white or yellow)
2 eggs
$^1/_2$ cup cocoa
2 Tbsp. water
2 Tbsp. cooking oil

Filling:

1 egg white, beaten
2 Tbsp. milk
$^1/_2$ cup Crisco
1 tsp. vanilla
1 Tbsp. flour
3 cups powdered sugar
$^1/_4$ tsp. salt

Let cake batter set 20 minutes (do not refrigerate). Shape into balls; flatten with bottom of glass, greased once and dipped into Nestle Quik or white sugar for each cookie. Bake at 300° for 8 minutes. When cool, frost and sandwich cookies.

Peanut Blossoms

$3^1/_2$ cups flour
2 tsp. baking soda
2 tsp. salt
1 cup sugar
1 cup brown sugar
1 cup shortening
1 cup peanut butter
2 eggs
4 Tbsp. milk
2 tsp. vanilla
Hershey's Kisses

Shape dough into balls. Roll in sugar; place on ungreased cookie sheet. Bake at 375°. After baking, immediately top each cookie with a Hershey's Kiss; press down firmly.

wooden spoon wisdom

A happy home is not one without
problems, but one that handles them
with understanding and love.

Whoopie Pies

Mrs. Alvin (Katie) Brenneman

2 cups sugar	³/₄ cup vegetable oil
2 tsp. baking powder	2 tsp. baking soda
2 tsp. vanilla	¹/₂ tsp. salt
2 eggs	³/₄–1 cup cocoa
1 cup water	1 cup buttermilk
bread flour to thicken	
(approx 4 cups)	

Mix in order given and place on cookie sheet with soup spoon. Bake in a hot oven. Do not overbake if you want a soft cookie. Leave cookies on sheet a few seconds before taking out of pan.

Icing:

1 cup egg whites	¹/₃–¹/₂ can Crisco
2 lb. powdered sugar	

Whip with potato masher for 10–20 minutes. This is enough icing for a double batch of Whoopie Pies.

miriam's memories

When Mom and her youngest sister Esther were little girls, their neighbors had a farm auction. So after school they were allowed to go to the auction. They also had a lunch stand, so of course they had to get something to eat. They both decided on a whoopie pie wrapped in plastic wrap. When Esther opened hers there was no frosting in the middle. Mom told her she should go and tell the people at the lunch stand and ask for another one. But she ate two dry cookies instead of the good whoopie pie cookie she thought she was getting.

Peanut Drop Cookies

2 cups brown sugar
1 cup shortening
1/2 tsp. salt
1 tsp. vanilla
2 eggs
2 cups flour

1 1/2 cups peanuts
1/2 tsp. baking soda
1 tsp. baking powder
1 cup crushed corn flakes
2 cups oatmeal

Drop by teaspoonfuls onto greased cookie sheet and bake at 350°.

Peanut Butter Cookies

1 cup shortening
1/2 tsp. salt
1 cup peanut butter
1 cup white sugar
1 cup brown sugar

2 eggs
1 Tbsp. milk
2 cups sifted flour
1 tsp. baking soda

Drop by teaspoonfuls onto greased cookie sheet. Press cookie lightly with fork to flatten. Bake at 325° for 15–20 minutes.

Chewy Oatmeal Cookies

1 cup brown sugar
1 cup butter
1 tsp. vanilla
1 egg
1 cup flour

1 tsp. baking soda
1/2 tsp. salt
2 cups quick oats
1/2 cup nuts
1 cup chocolate chips

Drop onto ungreased cookie sheet. Bake at 375° for 7–10 minutes.

Peanut Butter Cookies

Miss Barbara P. Hochstetler

1 cup white sugar
1 cup brown sugar
2/3 cup shortening
2 eggs
2 cups peanut butter

2 3/4 cups flour
4 tsp. baking powder
1/2 tsp. baking soda
1 tsp. vanilla

Mix in order given. Roll into small balls; place on cookie sheet. Flatten with potato masher. Bake at 325°.

Peanut Butter Cookies

½ cup white sugar
½ cup brown sugar
½ cup shortening
½ cup peanut butter
1 egg

1¼ cups flour
½ tsp. baking powder
¾ tsp. baking soda
¼ tsp. salt
jelly, jam, or frosting

Refrigerate 3 hours. Heat oven to 375°. Bake until set, but do not overbake. Cool slightly before removing from cookie sheet. Spread jelly, jam, or frosting between two cookies and press together.

Sorghum Cookies

Miss Sara Miller

2½ cups white sugar
2½ cups brown sugar
3 cups shortening
4 eggs
8 tsp. baking soda, dissolved
   in buttermilk

1 cup buttermilk
1 cup cane molasses
4 tsp. cinnamon
2 tsp. baking powder
1 tsp. salt
12 cups flour

Chill; shape into balls and roll in white sugar. Bake at 325°; do not overbake. Fill with Ho-Ho cake filling or cream stick filling.

Molasses Sugar Cookies

¾ cup shortening
1 cup sugar
1 egg
¼ cup molasses
2 cups flour

2 tsp. baking soda
¼ tsp. cloves
½ tsp. ginger
1 tsp. cinnamon
½ tsp. salt

Mix well, then chill. Make into balls; roll in granulated sugar and place on greased cookie sheet. Bake at 375° for 8–10 minutes.

Mother's Bell Collection

*N*ow let's go upstairs. Up and to the right is my
room. All of us children sleep upstairs.

In one corner of my room is
my Mother's bell collection. We
have more than just the six
you see here. When my
family travels, Mom tries
to buy a bell. Occasionally
we'll get one from my
relatives that know we
love bells.

Molasses Crinkle Cookies

Miss Fannie Miller

4 cups oleo	1 tsp. ginger
8 cups brown sugar	8 tsp. cinnamon
1 cup Brer Rabbit molasses (light)	2 tsp. salt
8 eggs	12 tsp. baking soda
1 cup sour cream	4 tsp. baking powder
16 cups flour	

Filling:

1 cup milk	1 cup sugar
2 Tbsp. cornstarch	$1/2$ cup Crisco
1 tsp. vanilla	$1/2$ cup oleo

Mix and refrigerate overnight. Shape into balls; roll in white sugar. Fill with filling.

Molasses Cookies

Miss Verna P. Hochstetler

$1^1/2$ cups shortening	1 tsp. cloves
2 cups sugar	1 tsp. ginger
$1/2$ cup baking molasses	2 tsp. cinnamon
2 eggs	1 tsp. salt
4 tsp. baking soda	4 cups flour

Melt shortening and cool; add sugar, molasses, and eggs, beating well. Sift baking soda, spices, and flour; add to first mixture. Chill. Form into small balls. Roll balls in white sugar and bake. I use half blackstrap and half light Karo for molasses.

Chewy Honey Cookies

1 cup brown sugar	$2^1/2$ cups flour
$3/4$ cup margarine	2 tsp. baking soda
1 egg	1 tsp. cinnamon
$1/3$ cup honey	$1/4$ tsp. salt

Chill. Shape into balls the size of walnuts. Dip tops in sugar and place on ungreased cookie sheet. Sprinkle each with 2–3 drops of water. Bake at 375° for 10 minutes. Cookies will flatten as they bake.

Honey Crunch Cookies

2 cups flour
$^1/_2$ tsp. salt
1 cup honey
1 cup shredded coconut
4 cups crispy rice cereal

2 tsp. baking powder
1 cup butter or margarine
2 eggs
1 cup butterscotch chips

Drop by teaspoonfuls onto greased cookie sheets. Bake at 350° for about 12 minutes, or until golden brown. Yield: about 5 dozen.

Butterscotch Pie Filling Cookies

Mrs. Ammon (Lydia) Miller

1 small box butterscotch instant
   pudding, dry
1 cup sugar
$^1/_2$ cup shortening
$^1/_2$ cup sour cream or milk
$2^1/_2$ cups flour

1 egg
pinch of salt
1 tsp. baking soda
1 tsp. baking powder
1 tsp. vanilla

Mix together and drop by teaspoonfuls onto greased cookie sheet.

Butterscotch Delight Cookies

$2^1/_2$ cups white sugar
$2^1/_2$ cups brown sugar
2 cups shortening
$2^1/_2$ tsp. baking soda
$2^1/_2$ tsp. baking powder
5 eggs

2 Tbsp. vanilla
$^1/_4$ cup milk
5 cups flour
2 tsp. salt
5 cups quick oatmeal

Form into balls; roll in powdered sugar and flatten slightly on baking sheet.

Butterscotch Cookies *Mrs. Eli (Verna) Miller*

2 cups white sugar
2 cups brown sugar
1 cup lard or Crisco
4 well-beaten eggs
1 tsp. salt
1 tsp. vanilla
$^1/_2$ cup hot water
1 rounded Tbsp. baking soda,
    dissolved in hot water
8 cups flour
1 Tbsp. baking powder

Mix together and drop by teaspoonfuls onto greased cookie sheet. Press down with potato masher. Dip potato masher in flour so it won't stick. Bake at 350°.

Little Debbie Cookies

1 cup oleo
3 cups brown sugar
3 cups oatmeal
4 eggs
2 tsp. cinnamon
$1^1/_2$ tsp. nutmeg
1 tsp. baking soda
3 cups flour

Filling:

2 egg whites
2 tsp. vanilla
4 Tbsp. milk
4 cups powdered sugar
1 cup Crisco

Shape into small balls and flatten on cookie sheet. Bake at 350°. Fill with filling.

Coconut Oatmeal Cookies

Mrs. John (Marie) Miller

2 cups shortening
2 cups brown sugar
2 cups white sugar
4 eggs
2 tsp. vanilla
5 cups oatmeal
2 cups coconut
3 $^1/_2$ cups flour
2 tsp. baking soda
2 tsp. baking powder
1 cup nuts
2 cups butterscotch chips

Bake at 350°.

Double Crunchers

Miss Betty M. Miller

1¹/₂ cups shortening
1¹/₂ cups brown sugar
1¹/₂ cups white sugar
3 eggs
1¹/₂ tsp. vanilla
³/₄ tsp. salt

1¹/₂ tsp. baking soda
1¹/₂ cups coconut
3 cups Rice Krispies
3 cups oatmeal
3¹/₂ cups flour

Chocolate Filling:

1 - 6 oz. pkg. chocolate chips
3 Tbsp. water

1¹/₂ cups powdered sugar
1 - 8 oz. pkg. cream cheese

Shape into balls; flatten with bottom of glass dipped in flour. Roll in powdered sugar, if desired. Bake 8–10 minutes at 350°. For Chocolate Filling, melt chocolate chips and add the rest.

Double Crunchers

1 egg
¹/₂ cup shortening
¹/₂ tsp. vanilla
¹/₂ cup brown sugar
¹/₂ cup white sugar
1 cup flour

¹/₂ tsp. baking soda
1 cup rolled oats
1 tsp. salt
1 cup coconut
1 cup corn flakes or Rice Krispies

Cream together egg, sugars, shortening, and vanilla. Add dry ingredients, coconut, and cereal. Flatten on cookie sheet. Bake at 350°.

Filling:

Melt ¹/₂ cup butterscotch chips in double boiler. Stir in ¹/₂ cup powdered sugar, 1 Tbsp. water, and ¹/₄ cup cream cheese. Spread between cookies to make sandwich cookies.

Bushel Cookies

5 lbs. brown sugar
12 eggs
2 lbs. raisins
1 cup maple syrup
5 cups lard or butter
1 qt. sweet milk

2 lbs. quick oatmeal
4 Tbsp. baking soda
4 Tbsp. baking powder
6 lbs. flour
1 lb. salted peanuts

Chocolate chips are good, too. They can be substituted for the raisins, or use half of each. Drop onto cookie sheets and bake. Yield: about 300 cookies.

106

Butterscotch Oatmeal Cookies

1 cup white sugar	$^1/_2$ cup nuts
1 cup brown sugar	1 cup coconut
1 cup shortening	1 tsp. baking soda
2 eggs	1 tsp. baking powder
2 cups flour	1 tsp. vanilla
2 $^1/_2$ cups oatmeal	1 cup butterscotch chips

Cream sugar and shortening; add eggs and vanilla; beat well. Add oatmeal and coconut, then stir in flour, baking soda, baking powder, nuts, and chips. Drop by teaspoonfuls onto greased cookie sheet. Bake at 375°.

Delicious Raisin Top Cookies

Mrs. Ben (Esther) Miller

2 cups brown sugar	4 or more cups flour
1 cup shortening	2 eggs
1 tsp. salt	1 tsp. soda
1 Tbsp. vanilla	4 Tbsp. milk

Dough should be stiff enough to roll into balls. Take thumb and make a hole in the cookie ball and put filling in the hole.

Filling:

1 cup raisins	$^3/_4$ cup sugar
2 cups water	pinch of salt
a little maple flavor	

Cook $^1/_2$ hour and thicken with 1 Tbsp. cornstarch.

wooden spoon wisdom

Do not be like the rooster who thought
the sun rose to hear him crow.

Delicious Oatmeal Cookies

Mrs. Alvin (Katie) Brenneman

3 cups brown sugar
1½ cups Crisco
3 eggs
1¼ tsp. vanilla
1¼ tsp. baking powder

2¼ cups flour
1¼ tsp. baking soda
¼ tsp. salt
4½ cups oatmeal

Cream sugar and Crisco. Add eggs and vanilla; beat well, then add dry ingredients. Form into balls and roll in powdered sugar. Flatten slightly. Bake at 325° for 8–10 minutes. Do not overbake.

Date Oatmeal Cookies

1¾ cups shortening
1 cup white sugar
1 cup brown sugar
4 eggs
1 cup buttermilk
2 tsp. soda
2 tsp. baking powder

2 tsp. salt
2 tsp. cinnamon
4 cups oatmeal
4 cups flour
1–1½ lb. dates
1½ cups water
nuts (if desired)

Cook dates in water.

Frosting:

Melt 1 stick butter. Blend in 1 cup brown sugar and ¼ tsp. salt. Cook this on low heat for 2 minutes, stirring constantly. Add ¼ cup milk or cream. Remove from heat and add powdered sugar as desired. Add vanilla and maple flavoring to suit your taste.

Pumpkin Chocolate Chip Cookies

1 cup butter or oleo, softened
¾ cup packed brown sugar
¾ cup white sugar
1 egg, beaten
1 tsp. vanilla extract
2 cups flour

1 cup quick cooking oats
1 tsp. baking soda
1 tsp. cinnamon
1 cup cooked or canned pumpkin
1½ cups chocolate chips

Drop by tablespoonfuls onto greased cookie sheet. Bake at 350° for 12 minutes.

Orange Cookies

Miss Elsie Miller

2 cups sugar
1 cup shortening
1 orange, ground fine
  (or $^2/_3$ cup orange juice)
1 cup sour cream

1 tsp. baking soda, dissolved in
  sour cream
2 tsp. baking powder
5 cups flour

Bake at 400°.

Frosting:

orange juice
powdered sugar

chunk of butter (if you like)

Pumpkin Cookies

1 cup shortening
2 cups brown sugar
2 cups pumpkin
4 cups flour

2 tsp. baking powder
2 tsp. baking soda
2 tsp. cinnamon

Mix and drop by spoonfuls onto greased cookie sheet. Bake in hot oven till brown. Ice with powdered sugar icing while still warm. (Good with or without nuts, dates, or raisins.)

Pineapple Cookies

2 eggs
1 cup brown sugar
1 cup white sugar
1 cup oleo
1 cup crushed pineapple, drained
2 tsp. vanilla

1 cup chopped nuts
4 cups flour
$^1/_2$ tsp. salt
$^1/_2$ tsp. baking soda
2 tsp. baking powder

Bake at 400° for 10–12 minutes.

wooden spoon wisdom

Any trouble that is too small to take to
God in prayer is too small to worry about.

Date Pinwheel Cookies

$^1/_2$ cup shortening	$^1/_2$ tsp. baking soda
2 cups brown sugar	$^1/_2$ tsp. salt
2 eggs, well beaten	$^1/_2$ tsp. cream of tartar
4 cups flour	1 tsp. vanilla

Filling:

$^1/_2$ lb. dates	$^1/_2$ cup nuts
$^1/_4$ cup water	$^1/_2$ cup white sugar

Cream shortening and sugar; add eggs. Add flour sifted with baking soda, salt, and cream of tartar. Stir well; add vanilla. Roll out and spread with filling. Roll as jelly roll. Keep in cool place overnight. Slice and bake.

Date Cookies

8 cups flour	1 tsp. salt
4 cups sugar	2 cups shortening
2 tsp. baking soda	6 large eggs
2 tsp. cream of tartar	

Filling:

2 Tbsp. cornstarch	2 cups brown sugar
2 cups water	Juice of 2 lemons or 2 Tbsp.
1 cup cut up dates	ReaLemon

Bake at 375°.

Banana Jumbos

1 cup soft shortening (part butter)	$1^1/_2$ tsp. salt
1 cup sugar	$^1/_2$ tsp. baking soda
2 eggs	1 cup chopped nuts
$^1/_2$ cup buttermilk	1 cup mashed, ripe bananas
3 cups flour	1 tsp. vanilla

Bake at 375° for about 10 minutes, until delicately browned. Yield: about $3^1/_2$ dozen.

Applesauce Cookies

$^1/_2$ cup shortening
$1^1/_3$ cups brown sugar
1 egg
1 cup applesauce
1 cup raisins
1 cup walnuts

$^1/_2$ tsp. nutmeg
$2^1/_4$ cups sifted flour
1 tsp. baking soda
$^1/_2$ tsp. cinnamon
$^1/_2$ tsp. cloves

Icing:

$^1/_4$ cup butter
$^1/_4$ cup brown sugar

$2^1/_2$ Tbsp. light cream
$1^1/_2$ cups powdered sugar

For icing, cook butter and sugar until sugar dissolves (about 3 minutes), then add remaining ingredients.

Jam Bars

2 cups rolled oats
$1^3/_4$ cups flour
1 cup shortening
1 cup brown sugar
$^1/_2$ cup chopped nuts

1 tsp. cinnamon
$^3/_4$ tsp. salt
$^1/_2$ tsp. baking soda
$^3/_4$ cup jam preserves (any flavor)

Combine all ingredients, except jam, in large bowl. Mix until mixture is crumbly. Reserve 2 cups mixture and press the rest in bottom of 13x9x2" baking pan. Spread jam evenly over mixture, then sprinkle with remaining mixture. Bake at 400° till golden brown. Cool and cut into squares.

Coffee Cookies

4 cups brown sugar
$1^3/_4$ cups lard
2 cups brewed coffee
4 eggs

2 tsp. vanilla
2 tsp. baking soda
6 tsp. baking powder
flour (till right, about $8^1/_2$ cups)

Mix; drop by teaspoonfuls onto greased cookie sheet. Bake at 350° for 10–15 minutes. Frost with caramel frosting.

Wyoming Whopper Cookies

³/₄ cup butter
³/₄ cup white sugar
1¹/₄ cups brown sugar
3 eggs, beaten
1¹/₂ cups chunky peanut butter

6 cups old-fashioned oats
2 tsp. baking soda
1¹/₂ cups raisins
1 pkg. chocolate chips

Melt butter over low heat. Blend in sugars, eggs, and peanut butter; mix until smooth. Add oats, baking soda, raisins, and chocolate chips. Mixture will be sticky. Drop onto greased baking sheet. Flatten slightly. Bake at 350° for about 15 minutes for large cookies.

Cinnamon Brownies

³/₄ cup baking cocoa
²/₃ cup butter or margine, melted
2 cups sugar
1 tsp. vanilla extract
1¹/₂–2 tsp. cinnamon
1 cup (6 oz.) chocolate chips

¹/₂ tsp. baking soda
¹/₂ cup boiling water
2 eggs, beaten
1¹/₃ cups flour
¹/₄ tsp. salt

Bake in a greased 13x9x2" pan at 350° for 40 minutes. Cool; frost with Chocolate Cinnamon Frosting.

Snickerdoodle Cookies

1¹/₂ cups shortening
1¹/₂ cups sugar
2 eggs
2³/₄ cups flour

2 tsp. cream of tartar
1 tsp. baking soda
¹/₂ tsp. salt

Chill dough. Make into balls; roll in mixture made of 2 Tbsp. sugar and 2 tsp. cinnamon. Place on ungreased cookie sheet. Do not flatten. Bake at 400° for 8–10 minutes, until lightly browned, but still soft.

Spellbinders

1 cup oleo, softened
1 cup brown sugar
1 egg
1 1/2 cups flour
1 cup nuts or chocolate chips

1/2 cup finely crushed corn flakes
1 cup oatmeal
1 tsp. soda
1 1/2 tsp. baking powder
1 cup coconut

Glaze:

2 Tbsp. butter or oleo, melted
1 cup powdered sugar

1 Tbsp. hot water
1/2 tsp. vanilla

Cream oleo and sugar; add egg. Add dry ingredients. Flatten with bottom of glass dipped in corn flakes. Bake at 350°.

Seven Layer Cookies

1 cup graham cracker crumbs
6 oz. chocolate chips
6 oz. butterscotch chips

1 cup coconut
1 cup chopped nuts
1 can Eagle Brand milk

Melt 1 stick oleo in 13x9x2" pan, then add each layer listed in order given. Do not stir. Bake at 325° for 25–30 minutes.

Double Treat Cookies

1 cup shortening
1 cup white sugar
1 cup brown sugar
1 cup peanut butter
2 eggs
1 Tbsp. vanilla

2 cups flour
1/2 tsp. salt
2 tsp. baking soda
3 cups quick oats
1 cup chopped nuts
1 cup chocolate chips

Shape into balls; place on cookie sheet. Flatten with glass dipped in sugar. Bake at 400°–425° for 6–8 minutes. If desired, dough can be spread in a thin layer on cookie sheet, then baked and cut into squares.

Potato Chip Cookies

1 cup oleo
1 cup brown sugar
1 cup white sugar
2 eggs
2 cups flour

$^1/_2$ tsp. salt
1 tsp. baking soda
1 tsp. vanilla
1 cup nuts
2 cups crushed potato chips

Bake at 350° for 12 minutes, or until done.

Spice Cookies

4 eggs
3 cups brown sugar
6 Tbsp. sour milk
$1^1/_4$ cups lard
5 cups flour (approx.)

2 tsp. baking soda
1 tsp. cinnamon
1 tsp. cloves
1 tsp. nutmeg

Drop by teaspoonfuls onto cookie sheet. Bake at 350°.

Jell-O Cookies

$^1/_2$ cup sugar
$2^3/_4$ cups flour
1 tsp. baking soda
$^1/_2$ cup butter
$^1/_2$ tsp. vanilla extract

$^1/_2$ tsp. salt
$^1/_2$ cup milk
2 eggs
3 oz. Jell-O (any flavor)

Drop onto ungreased cookie sheet. Bake at 350°. They're good with powdered sugar frosting with the same flavor of Jell-O.

Everything Cookies

$^1/_2$ cup oleo
1 cup brown sugar
1 cup white sugar
2 eggs
1 tsp. cream of tartar
1 cup oatmeal
$^1/_2$ cup salad oil

2 Tbsp. vanilla
1 tsp. salt
1 tsp. baking powder
3 cups flour
1 cup crispy rice cereal
1 cup chocolate chips or M&Ms

Drop onto ungreased cookie sheet. Bake at 350° until golden brown.

Lollipop Cookies

1 cup flour
1/2 cup sugar
1 tsp. baking powder
1/4 tsp. salt
1/2 cup packed brown sugar
1/2 cup shortening
1 egg, beaten
1 tsp. vanilla

1 tsp. water
1 cup oatmeal
Popsicle sticks
frosting
coconut
jelly beans
licorice

Shape dough into 24 balls. Place on ungreased cookie sheet. Flatten with the bottom of a glass dipped in flour. Insert a Popsicle stick in each, if desired. Bake at 350° for 8–10 minutes. Remove from the cookie sheet and cool. Decorate with frosting, coconut, and candies to make faces.

Coconut Macaroon Cookies

Mrs. Raymond (Anna Mae) Troyer

1 cup white sugar
1 cup brown sugar
1 cup margarine
1 cup Wesson or vegetable oil
2 eggs

4 1/2 cups flour
1 tsp. cream of tartar
1 tsp. baking soda
1 tsp. vanilla
1 tsp. salt

Combine first 4 ingredients; beat well. Add eggs; beat well. Add remaining ingredients. For coconut cookie, add 1 cup coconut and 2 tsp. coconut flavor. Frost with your favorite frosting. (We like them well for sandwich cookies, or just frosted on top.)

Soft Sugar Cookies

Miss Katie Miller

1 lb. shortening
3 cups white sugar
4 eggs
2 cups evaporated milk or
    sweet cream

8–10 cups flour
1/2 tsp. salt
2 tsp. baking soda
6 tsp. baking powder

Cream shortening and sugar; add eggs and beat well. Add cream and dry ingredients. Roll out or drop onto greased cookie sheet. Bake at 400° for 6 minutes, or until done. Do not overbake or they won't be soft. Lemon flavoring can be added.

Ranger Cookies

Miss Wilma Miller

1 cup shortening
2 cups flour
1 cup brown sugar
2 eggs
1 tsp. vanilla
$^1/_2$ cup chocolate chips
1 tsp. baking soda

$^1/_2$ tsp. baking powder
$^1/_2$ cup white sugar
2 cups Rice Krispies
2 cups oatmeal
1 cup coconut
$^1/_2$ cup nuts

Mix in order given. Roll into balls and flatten with fork. Bake on greased cookie sheet until lightly browned.

Frosted Cream Cookies (Molasses)

2 cups baking molasses
2 cups shortening
1 cup sugar
$^1/_2$ cup water

1 Tbsp. baking soda
3 eggs
flour to roll dough out easily

Frosting:

$1^3/_4$ cups sugar

4 Tbsp. water

For frosting, boil till it threads. Pour over 2 beaten egg whites. Beat until smooth. Add vanilla. Spread on cookies.

Delicious Cookies

1 cup brown sugar
1 cup white sugar
1 cup soft oleo
1 cup vegetable oil
1 egg
2 tsp. vanilla
$3^1/_2$ cups flour
M&Ms

1 tsp. cream of tartar
1 tsp. baking powder
$^1/_2$ tsp. salt
1 cup Rice Krispies
1 cup nuts
1 cup oatmeal
1 cup coconut

Mix in order given. Shape into balls; flatten with fork. Bake at 350° for 10 minutes.

Caramel Cookies

2 cups brown sugar
1 cup shortening
5 cups flour

4 eggs
1 tsp. baking soda
1 tsp. cream of tartar

Cream sugar and shortening together. Add eggs, one at a time, beating well after each addition. Add dry ingredients; mix well. Make into a roll. Chill overnight. Slice and bake at 350°.

Crisp Energy Cookies

1 cup white sugar
1 cup brown sugar
1 tsp. vanilla
1 cup shortening
2 eggs
2 cups flour
1 tsp. salt
1 tsp. baking powder

1 tsp. baking soda
1 tsp. cinnamon
2 cups crispy rice cereal
2 cups oatmeal
$^3/_4$ cup raisins
$^1/_2$ cup coconut
$^1/_2$ cup chopped walnuts

Chill 1–2 hours. Roll into walnut-size balls and bake on ungreased cookie sheet at 350° for 12–15 minutes.

Cream Wafers

2 beaten eggs
1 cup sugar
$^1/_2$ cup butter or lard
2 Tbsp. cream

$1^1/_2$ tsp. baking soda
1 tsp. vanilla
$^1/_2$ tsp. cinnamon
$^1/_2$ tsp. salt

Add enough flour to make a stiff dough. Roll out real thin or use cookie press.

Never Fail Cupcakes

1 egg
$^1/_2$ cup cocoa
$^1/_2$ cup butter or oleo, melted
$1^1/_2$ cups flour

$^1/_2$ cup sour milk
1 tsp. baking soda
1 cup sugar
$^1/_2$ cup hot water

Put in bowl in order given. Do not mix until everything is in bowl. Bake at 350° for 15–20 minutes. Frost when cool.

Baked Apple Donuts

4¹/₂ cups flour
1¹/₂ tsp. nutmeg (optional)
1¹/₂ tsp. salt
3 eggs, beaten
³/₄ cup milk

³/₄ tsp. baking powder
1¹/₂ cups sugar
1 cup shortening
1¹/₂ cups grated raw apples

For Coating:

³/₄ cup melted oleo
1 cup sugar

3 tsp. cinnamon

Stir together flour, baking powder, nutmeg, sugar, and salt. Cut in shortening. Combine eggs, milk, and apples; add to crumb mixture. Mix quickly until thoroughly blended. Fill greased muffin cups ³/₄ full. Bake at 350° for 20–25 minutes. Remove from pans and roll in melted margarine (while still warm), then in mixture of 1 cup sugar and 3 tsp. cinnamon.

A.M. Delight Muffins   *Miss Rachel Weaver*

2 cups all-purpose flour
³/₄ cup sugar
2 tsp. baking soda
1¹/₂ tsp. ground cinnamon
¹/₂ tsp. salt
3 eggs
¹/₂ cup applesauce

¹/₂ cup milk
1¹/₂ tsp. vanilla extract
2 cups chopped, peeled apples
2 cups grated carrots
¹/₂ cup flaked coconut
¹/₂ cup raisins
¹/₂ cup sliced almonds

In a large bowl, combine flour, sugar, baking soda, cinnamon, and salt. In another bowl, beat eggs; add applesauce, milk, and vanilla. Mix well; stir into dry ingredients just until moistened. Fold in the remaining ingredients. Fill greased or paper-lined muffin cups ³/₄ full. Bake at 375° for 20–25 minutes, or until muffins test done.

wooden spoon wisdom

You are never fully dressed in the
morning until you put on a smile.

Fruit and Nut Muffins

4 cups diced, peeled tart baking
    apples ($^1/_4$" pieces)
1 cup sugar
$1^1/_2$ cups raisins
$1^1/_2$ cups chopped nuts
2 eggs

$^1/_2$ cup vegetable oil
2 tsp. vanilla extract
2 cups all-purpose flour
$1^1/_2$ tsp. baking soda
2 tsp. ground cinnamon
$^1/_8$ tsp. salt

In a large mixing bowl, combine apples, sugar, raisins, and nuts; set aside. In another bowl, beat eggs, oil, and vanilla. Stir into apple mixture. Combine dry ingredients; carefully fold into apple mixture. Do not overmix. Fill 18 greased muffin cups almost to the top. Bake at 375° for 18–20 minutes, or until muffins test done. Yield: $1^1/_2$ dozen.

Cinnamon Doughnut Muffins

$1^3/_4$ cups flour
$1^1/_2$ tsp. baking powder
$^1/_2$ tsp. salt
$^1/_4$ tsp. cinnamon
$^1/_2$ tsp. nutmeg

$^3/_4$ cup sugar
$^1/_3$ cup vegetable oil
1 egg, lightly beaten
$^3/_4$ cup milk

Topping:

$^1/_4$ cup butter, melted
$^1/_3$ cup sugar

1 tsp. cinnamon

In a large bowl, combine flour, baking powder, salt, nutmeg, and cinnamon. Combine sugar, oil, egg, and milk; stir into dry ingredients until just moistened. Fill greased or paper-lined muffin cups $^1/_2$ full (10 muffin cups). Place 1 teaspoon jam on top. Cover with enough batter to fill muffin cups $^3/_4$ full. Bake at 350° for 20–25 minutes.

For Topping: Place melted butter in a bowl; combine sugar and cinnamon in another bowl. Immediately after removing muffins from the oven, dip tops in melted butter, then in cinnamon and sugar.

Sugarless Fruit-Nut Muffins

Mrs. Ivan A. Miller

1 cup chopped dates
$^1/_2$ cup raisins
$^1/_2$ cup chopped prunes
1 cup water
$^1/_2$ cup oleo
$^1/_4$ tsp. salt

2 eggs, beaten
1 tsp. vanilla
1 cup flour
1 tsp. baking soda
$^1/_2$ cup chopped nuts

Combine dates, raisins, prunes, and water in saucepan. Bring to a boil and boil 5 minutes. Stir in oleo and salt; cool. Add remaining ingredients to fruit; stir just until dry ingredients are moistened. Bake at 350° for 20 minutes, or until done.

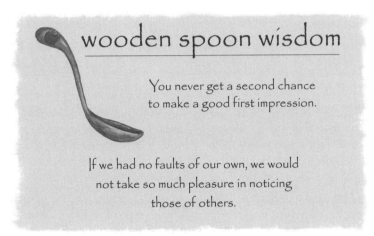

wooden spoon wisdom

You never get a second chance
to make a good first impression.

If we had no faults of our own, we would
not take so much pleasure in noticing
those of others.

Desserts

The famous pudding
   You've heard about
Is the wedding dessert,
   Date Pudding, no doubt.

I'm sure you'd agree
   That my mom makes the best,
If you'd come one day
   And be our dinner guest.

It also looks so nice
   Layered in a huge bowl.
To make it taste good
   And also be pretty—that's
     her goal!

It's almost too pretty
   To dig in and eat.
But I still say
   Mom's Date Pudding
     can't be beat!

DESSERTS MINI INDEX

DESSERTS MINI INDEX

wooden spoon wisdom

The woods would be very silent if no birds
sang except the ones who sang the best.

Cats have kittens,
Fish have little fishes,
So why can't sinks have little sinks
Instead of dirty dishes?

Some people are like buttons—
Popping off at the wrong time.

Happiness is a perfume you cannot
pour on others without getting
a few drops on yourself.

Another Day

*I*t's early morning. Mom calls upstairs with her cheerful wakeup call: "Miriam, time to get up and start washing!"

I stretch and yawn. Then again. And again. Finally I part with my warm bed and sleepily rub my eyes and reach for the matches on the nightstand. Mom still cooks with a cookstove. I light my room with an oil lamp.

The floor is cold. I dress quickly and start downstairs.

Oh, I forgot to snuff out my oil lamp. My day begins.

Banana Split Pizza

14 oz. Eagle Brand sweetened
    condensed milk
$^1/_2$ cup sour cream
6 Tbsp. lemon juice, divided
1 tsp. vanilla
$^1/_2$ cup margarine, softened
$^1/_4$ cup brown sugar
1 cup flour

$^1/_4$ cup rolled oats
$^1/_2$ cup chopped pecans, divided
3 sliced bananas, divided
8 oz. pineapple tidbits
maraschino cherries
$^1/_2$ cup chocolate chips
1 Tbsp. Crisco

Preheat oven to 375°. Combine milk, sour cream, $^1/_4$ cup lemon juice, and vanilla; chill. Beat margarine and sugar. Add flour, oats, and $^1/_4$ cup pecans. Press dough into an ungreased pizza pan and prick with fork. Bake for 10–12 minutes; cool. Arrange 2 sliced bananas over top of crust. Spoon on filling and spread evenly. Dip remaining banana in remaining 2 Tbsp. of lemon juice. Arrange on top with pineapple, cherries, and remaining nuts. Melt chocolate chips with Crisco and drizzle over top.

Fruit Pizza

First Layer:

$^3/_4$ cup brown sugar
1 egg, beaten
$^1/_2$ cup oleo, melted
1 tsp. vanilla

1 tsp. lemon flavoring
1 tsp. baking powder
1$^1/_4$ cups flour

Second Layer:

8 oz. Cool Whip
8 oz. cream cheese

$^3/_4$ cup powdered sugar

Mix and spread first layer on 13x17" pizza pan. Bake at 300° for 20 minutes. Mix second layer and spread on first layer. Third layer is fruit of your choice (apples, nuts, pineapple, and grapes). Take juice of pineapple and add $^3/_4$ cup water, 2 Tbsp. clear jel, and $^3/_4$ cup sugar; heat and bring to a boil. When cold, pour over fruit; mix all together and pour over second layer.

Fruit Slush

Miss Leanna Miller

1 qt. peaches
6 oz. frozen orange juice
6 sliced bananas

1 can crushed pineapple
3 cups water
2 cups sugar

Mix orange juice as directed. Mix and freeze. Thaw to slush to serve.

Summer Dessert

1 qt. water
$\frac{1}{2}$ cup clear jel

$1\frac{1}{2}$ cups sugar
1 pkg. orange Kool-Aid

Cook together and cool, then add fruit to your taste or liking.

Cool Whip Salad

Mrs. Wayne Hershberger

In a large bowl, mix:
1 cup white sugar

1 large can crushed pineapple

In a saucepan, mix:
6 Tbsp. cold water (plus)

2 pkg. Knox gelatine

Bring to a boil. Pour over sugar and pineapple and stir.

Get ready:
2 large carrots, shredded
1 cup chopped celery
1 cup cottage cheese

1 cup nuts
1 large container Cool Whip
$1\frac{1}{2}$ cups Hellman's mayonnaise

Mix with mixture in bowl and let set.

wooden spoon wisdom

If you have an unpleasant neighbor,
chances are he does too.

Oven-Baked Caramel Apples

10 apples
$^1/_4$ cup butter, melted
1 cup brown sugar

2 Tbsp. flour
1 cup water

Core and pare apples, then arrange in a greased baking dish. In a small saucepan, combine butter, sugar, and flour. Cook, stirring occasionally, until mixture is caramelized. Add water; bring mixture to a boil. Continue boiling until thick. Pour mixture over apples and bake at 350° until apples are still firm, but tender. Place 1 large marshmallow in center of each apple. Continue baking until marshmallow is lightly browned. Serve hot with whipped cream and chopped nuts.

Butterscotch Apples

$1^1/_2$ cups brown sugar
3 Tbsp. flour

butter size of a walnut

Put a dot of butter on each apple. Mix flour and sugar with water. Pour over apples and bake at 350° until apples are tender.

Skillet Apples

4 cooking apples, peeled and sliced
2 Tbsp. butter
$^1/_2$ cup sugar

1 tsp. cinnamon
2 Tbsp. cornstarch
$1^1/_2$ cups water

Combine all ingredients and cook in skillet for about 20 minutes.

Cinnamon Candy Salad

1 pkg. cherry Jell-O
1 cup hot water
$^1/_4$ cup red hots
$^1/_2$ cup boiling water

1 cup chopped apples
1 cup chopped celery
$^1/_2$ cup chopped nuts

Dissolve Jell-O in 1 cup water. Add red hots to $^1/_2$ cup boiling water; stir to dissolve. Add enough water to make 1 cup liquid; add to dissolved Jell-O. Cool until partially set. Add remaining ingredients. Pour into mold.

Broken Glass Dessert

24 graham crackers, crushed
$^1/_2$ cup sugar
$^1/_2$ cup butter, melted
1 pkg. lemon Jell-O
1 pkg. lime Jell-O

1 pkg. strawberry Jell-O
1 pkg. unflavored gelatine
$^1/_4$ cup cold water
1 cup hot pineapple juice
1 pt. whipping cream

Combine crackers, sugar, and butter. Place half of this in a 13x9x2" pan. Reserve the remaining half for garnish. Dissolve each package of Jell-O in $1^1/_2$ cups hot water. Place in flat pan and allow to set until firm. Cut the Jell-O in squares. Dissolve gelatine in cold water; add pineapple juice. Add 1 Tbsp. sugar. Cool mixture to syrupy consistency. Add whipped cream. Add the Jell-O squares to the mixture and place in a pan. Garnish with reserved crumbs.

Apple Salad

Miss Ella A. Brenneman

2 boxes lemon Jell-O, mixed
   as directed
1 medium size can crushed
   pineapple, drained

3 diced apples
3 bananas

Topping:
$^1/_2$ cup pineapple juice
1 Tbsp. cornstarch

$^1/_2$ cup sugar

Cook topping till thick; cool. Mix together 1 envelope Dream Whip or 1 cup whipping cream. Put crushed nuts on top.

Pineapple Cheese Salad

Pour $3^1/_2$ cups boiling water over $^3/_4$ cup orange or pineapple Jell-O. Add 40 marshmallows and 8 oz. cream cheese to hot Jell-O. Let melt, then beat with beater till smooth. Set aside until it starts to thicken. Add 2 cups crushed pineapple, $^3/_4$ cup nuts, and 2 cups whipped cream. Pour into serving dish. Dissolve $^3/_4$ cup cherry Jell-O in 2 cups hot water. Stir till dissolved. Add 2 cups cold water. Let set till cold, then pour over salad.

Pretzel Salad

2 cups crushed pretzels $^3/_4$ cup melted oleo
  (not too fine)   3 tsp. sugar

Mix:

8 oz. cream cheese   1 cup sugar
1 - 9 oz. container Cool Whip

Mix together and bake in 13x9x2" pan. Bake 8 minutes at 400°. Spread cream cheese mixture on cooled pretzels. Mix together 2 small boxes strawberry Jell-O, 2 cups boiling water and 2 - 10 oz. pkgs. strawberries. Put this on top of cream cheese.

Crust Salad

Miss Lydia Troyer

2 cups Pillsbury flour $^1/_4$ cup brown sugar
1 cup chopped nuts $^1/_4$ cup oleo or butter

Press in pan and bake at 350° for 15–20 minutes. Drain the juice of a #202 can of crushed pineapple. Heat the juice. Put in 1 pkg. lime Jell-O; cool. Cream 8 oz. cream cheese and 1 cup white sugar. Blend in Jell-O and add pineapple; chill. Beat 1 can Pet milk. Mix all together and pour on top of crust. Some lime Jell-O may be put on top.

Crust Salad

Mix together:

2 cups flour   1 cup finely chopped nuts
$^1/_2$ cup brown sugar $^3/_4$ cup melted margarine

Press into 13x9x2" pan. Bake at 350° for 15 minutes; cool. Bring to a boil a 15 oz. can pineapple, undrained. Stir to dissolve 6 oz. lime Jell-O. Cool.

Cream:

$^3/_4$ cup sugar   8 oz. cream cheese

Fold cream cheese mixture into cooled gelatin mixture along with 4 cups whipped cream. Pour on cooled crust. Refrigerate. This crust is also very good to use for delight puddings, etc.

Orange Ring Salad

6 oz. orange Jell-O	11 oz. mandarin oranges
2 cups hot water	2 oz. crushed pineapple
2 cups orange sherbet	

Drain, then add half of the oranges and pineapple to the first 3 ingredients. Combine reserved juice and $^1/_2$ cup water and clear jel. Cool; add 4 oz. whipped topping and fruit.

Triple Orange Salad

1 box orange Jell-O	1 box tapioca pudding
1 box instant pudding	1 can mandarin oranges

Add $3^1/_2$ cups water to first 3 ingredients. Bring to a boil. Cool, then add mandarin oranges. Add Rich's topping when ready to serve.

Ribbon Salad

Bottom:

1 pkg. lime Jell-O	$^1/_2$ cup nuts
1 small can crushed pineapple	

Center:

1 pkg. lemon Jell-O	8 oz. cream cheese

Mix together. When cool, add $^3/_4$ cup whipped cream.

Top:

1 box red Jell-O, mixed as directed on box.

Let each layer set before adding next one.

wooden spoon wisdom

No one is so deaf as the person
who will not listen.

Indiana Salad

1st Layer:

1 cup lime Jell-O
2 cups hot water
1^1/$_2$ cups cold water

1 can crushed pineapple
1^1/$_2$ cups cold water

2nd Layer:

8 oz. cream cheese

1^1/$_2$ cups Rich's topping

3rd Layer:

2 cups pineapple
4 egg yolks
1^1/$_4$ cups sugar

3 Tbsp. clear jel
pinch of salt

Mini Cherry Cheesecakes

1 cup vanilla wafer crumbs
3 Tbsp. butter or oleo, melted
8 oz. cream cheese, softened
1^1/$_2$ tsp. vanilla

2 tsp. lemon juice
^{1}/$_3$ cup sugar
1 egg

Topping:

1 lb. pitted tart red cherries
^{1}/$_2$ cup sugar

2 Tbsp. cornstarch
red food coloring, optional

In a bowl, combine crumbs and butter. Press gently into the bottom of 12 paper-lined muffin cups. In a mixing bowl, combine cream cheese, vanilla, lemon juice, sugar, and egg. Beat until smooth; spoon into crusts. Bake at 375° for 12–15 minutes, or until set. Cool completely. Drain cherries, reserving ^{1}/$_2$ cup juice in a saucepan; discard remaining juice. To juice add cherries, sugar, cornstarch, and food coloring, if desired. Bring to a boil, stirring occasionally; boil for 1 minute. Cool; spoon over cheesecakes.

wooden spoon wisdom

The greatest of all faults
is to imagine you have none.

Coconut Cream Dessert *Miss Erma U. Weaver*

1 cup flour
1/4 cup brown sugar

1/2 cup butter or oleo
1 cup coconut

Mix well together and spread this crumbly mixture on cookie sheet. Bake at 350° until brown, stirring occasionally. Using your favorite vanilla pudding, put layers of cooked pudding and crumbs in a glass dish. Whipped cream and bananas may be added.

Sweetheart Pudding

2 1/2 cups graham cracker crumbs
1/2 cup sugar

2/3 cup melted butter

Mix and line bottom and sides of pan. Save 1 cup crumbs for topping. Make a filling with the following:

1 cup sugar
3 egg yolks
3 Tbsp. flour

4 cups milk
1 tsp. vanilla

Cook until thick and pour into crust. Beat 3 egg whites till stiff. Add 3 Tbsp. sugar and beat again. Pour over filling. Last, add reserved crumbs. Bake till brown. Cool before serving.

Orange Jell-O Dessert (Tapioca)

4 cups water
1/2 cup pearl tapioca
pinch of salt
1 pkg. orange Jell-O
1 tsp. Kool-Aid

2/3 cup sugar
4 oranges, cut up and mixed
  with sugar
1/2 cup sugar
whipped cream

Bring water to a boil; add tapioca and salt. Boil 10 minutes, stirring often. Remove from heat. Add Jell-O, Kool-Aid, and sugar. When cold, add oranges and whipped cream.

Cherry Delight

18 graham crackers, crushed
3 Tbsp. sugar
1/4 cup melted butter
8 oz. cream cheese

1 cup powdered sugar
1 cup whipped cream
1 can cherry pie filling

Mix first 3 ingredients and press in bottom of pan. Mix next 3 ingredients and pour over crust. Pour pie filling on top. Other pie fillings can be used, too.

Chocolate Eclair Pudding

2 sm. boxes instant vanilla pudding
3 cups milk
8 oz. cream cheese

1 cup whipped cream
whole graham crackers

Mix pudding and milk. Fold in softened cream cheese and whipped cream. Line a 13x9x2" pan with graham crackers. Put half of pudding on top. Add another layer of graham crackers. Put the rest of pudding on top, then layer of crackers. Mix and pour over crackers: 3 Tbsp. cocoa, 3 Tbsp. milk, 1 tsp. vanilla, and 1 1/2 cups powdered sugar. Best if chilled 2 hours.

Butterscotch Tapioca

6 cups boiling water
1 tsp. salt

1 1/2 cups pearl tapioca

Cook 15 minutes. Add 2 cups brown sugar. Cook till done (stir often).

Mix together:
2 beaten eggs
1/2 cup white sugar

1 cup milk

Add this to tapioca mixture. Cook until it bubbles. Brown 1 stick butter; add 1 tsp. vanilla. Cool and add whipped cream, bananas, and diced Snickers candy bar, if desired.

Pinescotch Pudding

2 eggs, beaten
1 cup sugar
1 cup crushed pineapple
1 cup nuts

3/4 cup flour
1 tsp. baking powder
1/4 tsp. salt

Sauce:

1/4 cup butter
1/4 cup pineapple juice
1/4 cup water

1 cup brown sugar
1 egg

Bake like a cake. When cold, cut into small squares. To make sauce, cook all ingredients together for several minutes. When cold, add whipped cream. Fix in layers with cake pieces like date pudding. Put whipped cream on top, if desired.

Vanilla Pudding or Pie Filling

6 1/2 cups milk, divided
6 Tbsp. cornstarch
2 cups sugar

2 eggs
pinch of salt
1 tsp. vanilla

Heat 6 cups milk to a boil. Mix the rest of the ingredients with remaining 1/2 cup of milk. Add to boiling milk. Bring to a boil again. Remove from heat; add vanilla. This is excellent for graham cracker pudding. Peanut butter, bananas, or coconut can be added, if desired.

Cottage Cheese Salad

1 box lime Jell-O
1 cup hot water
1 cup crushed pineapple

1 cup cottage cheese
1/2 cup Carnation milk
1/4 cup Miracle Whip

Dissolve Jell-O in hot water and chill. Whip Carnation milk and add Miracle Whip. When Jell-O is just starting to set, add pineapples, cottage cheese, and milk and Miracle Whip mixture. Add nuts, if desired.

Date Pudding

Mrs. Ivan A. Miller

1 cup dates, chopped
1 tsp. baking soda
1 cup white sugar
1 cup boiling water

1 Tbsp. butter
1 egg, beaten
1 cup flour
nuts (if desired)

Put dates, baking soda, and sugar in bowl. Pour boiling water over it. Add butter. Let set till cool. Add egg and flour. Bake in 13x9x2" pan at 400°. When cold, cut or break into small pieces and fill a serving bowl alternately with layers of cake pieces, bananas, and sweetened whipped cream. Vanilla or butterscotch pudding added to layers is good.

Punch Bowl Cake

1 box yellow cake mix
1 lg. box instant vanilla pudding
1 qt. fresh strawberries, sliced
20 oz. crushed pineapple

6 bananas
1 lg. container Cool Whip
1 cup chopped pecans

Bake the cake according to directions in a 13x9x2" pan; cool. Prepare the pudding according to directions. Crumble half of the cake in the bottom of a punch bowl. Add half of the next three ingredients: pudding, strawberries, and pineapple. Slice 3 bananas over top. Cover with half of the Cool Whip and sprinkle with half of the pecans. Repeat the layers again. This is very pretty and feeds a lot of people.

Graham Cracker Fluff

2 egg yolks
1 cup white sugar
1/2 cup milk
1 env. gelatin, mixed with 1/2 cup
  cold water

2 beaten egg whites
1 cup whipped cream
16 graham crackers, mixed with
  1/4 cup butter

Boil egg yolks, sugar, and milk 1 minute. Pour gelatin in hot water. Cool until it starts to set, then add rest of ingredients. Put in layers like graham cracker pudding.

Pineapple Pudding

1 large can pineapple
2 Tbsp. flour
salt
2 eggs, beaten

2 oranges
24 marshmallows
1 cup whipped cream
1 cup nuts

Drain juice from pineapples and place in double boiler. When hot, add sugar, flour, salt, and eggs. Cook until thick. When cooled, add cut up pineapples, oranges, marshmallows, whipped cream, and nuts.

Quick Butterscotch Dessert

Mrs. Ivan A. Miller

Mix butterscotch instant pudding according to directions. Add Ritz or graham crackers (broken into pieces), butterscotch chips, miniature marshmallows, nuts, and fresh apples (diced). Mix all together; top with whipped topping, if desired.

Pink Cloud

20 oz. lite cherry pie filling
20 oz. crushed pineapple, drained
8 oz. lite Cool Whip

14 oz. Eagle Brand milk
3 oz. cherry Jell-O (dry)
1/2 cup chopped nuts

Mix all together and refrigerate several hours before serving.

Butterfinger Dessert

60 Ritz crackers
1 stick butter, melted
6 oz. instant vanilla pudding
2 cups milk

1 qt. vanilla ice cream, softened
frozen whipped topping
3 Butterfinger candy bars

Crush crackers and mix with butter. Press into a 13x9x2" pan. Mix pudding with milk; add softened ice cream and beat. Pour into pan and chill. Next, spread whipped topping over mixture. Chop candy bars and sprinkle over top.

Snickers Dessert

Mrs. Raymond (Anna Mae) Troyer

2 cups flour
1 cup margarine
$^1/_2$ cup powdered sugar

1 - 6 oz. pkg. instant pudding
12–16 oz. whipped topping
5 chopped Snickers bars

Mix first three ingredients; sprinkle (do not press) into a 13x9x2" pan. Bake at 350° for 30 minutes. Cool completely. Mix pudding according to package directions; let set. Fold in topping and chopped candy bars. Pour into crust and chill.

Spanish Cream Pudding

Mrs. Aden (Sarah) Miller

$^2/_3$ cup water
2 pkgs. gelatin
2 cups white sugar

1 cup milk
4 egg yolks

Boil 1 minute; cool and add 4 egg whites and 2 cups cream or 1 can evaporated milk. Makes a big dish full.

Florida Pudding

Crust:

1 cup flour
$^1/_2$ cup chopped nuts

$^1/_2$ cup oleo

2nd Layer:

1 cup powdered sugar
8 oz. cream cheese

1 cup Cool Whip

3rd Layer:

Mix 3 cups milk with 2 boxes instant vanilla or butterscotch pudding.

Mix first 3 ingredients and press in bottom of a 12x8x2" baking pan. Bake at 350° till brown, then cool. Spread 2nd layer over cooled crust. Beat pudding and milk till thick, then spread on top of second layer and sprinkle with nuts.

Cinnamon Pudding

Step 1:

2 cups brown sugar
$1^1/2$ cups cold water
Mix and heat to boiling.

2 Tbsp. butter

Step 2:

1 cup sugar
2 Tbsp. butter
1 cup milk

$1^2/3$ cups flour
2 tsp. baking powder
2 tsp. cinnamon

Put Step 1 in bottom of pan, then put Step 2 in and sprinkle nuts on top. Bake 45 minutes, or until done. Top with whipped cream.

Peach Cake Dessert

1 yellow cake mix
1 cup chopped peaches
1 cup water (can use part peach juice)

$1/2$ cup oil
2 eggs

Streusel:

$1^1/2$ cup brown sugar
$1/2$ cup chopped nuts

2 tsp. cinnamon

Put half of batter in 13x9x2" pan. Sprinkle half of streusel, then rest of batter. Top with streusel. Bake at 350° for 25–30 minutes. Serve this with peach topping made from 1 cup of chopped peaches and peach juice thickened with clear jel or cornstarch. Can also serve this as coffee cake without the peach topping.

Cinnamon Bread Pudding

3 eggs
1 cup half and half
$1/2$ cup sugar
3 Tbsp. butter
1 tsp. vanilla

$1/2$ cup raisins
$1/2$ cup walnuts, chopped
1 loaf cinnamon bread, crusts
  removed and sliced into 2" cubes
cinnamon to sprinkle

In a large mixing bowl, beat eggs, half and half, and sugar. Add butter, vanilla, rasins, and walnuts; set aside. Grease a 13x9x2" baking dish. Fill dish with bread. Pour wet mixture over bread and mix lightly. Sprinkle cinnamon on top. Bake at 350° for about 30 minutes.

Oreo Dessert

46 Oreo cookies
$^1/_2$ cup butter
$^1/_2$ gal. ice cream

1 - 8 oz. container Cool Whip
1 sm. can chocolate syrup
$^1/_2$ cup chopped pecans

Combine cookies and melted butter. Spread in bottom of 13x9x2" pan, reserving $^1/_2$ cup for top. Spread softened ice cream over crumbs. Spread chocolate syrup over ice cream. Cover with Cool Whip. Sprinkle with chopped pecans and reserved cookie crumbs. Freeze.

Oreo Cookie Dessert   *Miss Clara Hershberger*

15 oz. Oreo cookies
8 oz. cream cheese
1 - 3 oz. pkg. instant chocolate
    pudding

1 - 3 oz. pkg. vanilla pudding
1 lg. container Cool Whip

Mix chocolate pudding with 2 cups milk. Do this first so the pudding will be firm enough to spread.

1st Layer: Smash the Oreos into little bits. Save some for top. Put the rest in bottom of pan.

2nd Layer: Mix the Cool Whip, vanilla pudding, and cream cheese together. Spread half of this mixture on top of the first layer.

3rd Layer: Chocolate pudding mixture.

4th Layer: Rest of Cool Whip mixture.

5th Layer: Sprinkle rest of crumbs on top. Refrigerate several hours. Can be made the day before.

Oreo Cookie Dessert   *Mrs. Ammon (Lydia) Miller*

1 pkg. Oreo cookies, crushed
1 - 8 oz. pkg. cream cheese

1 cup powdered sugar
2 cups whipped cream

Cream together cream cheese and powdered sugar. Add whipped cream. Cook vanilla pudding and add to creamed mixture. Line bottom of pan with some of the crushed cookies. Put filling on top and top with more crushed cookies.

Pie Filling Pudding
Mrs. Ammon (Lydia) Miller

1 can pie filling (any flavor)
1 box cake mix
1 stick oleo

Place pie filling in bottom of greased pan, then pour cake mix over filling. Melt oleo and put on top. Bake at 325° for 1 hour. Good with whipped cream on top.

Fruit Crumble
Mrs. John (Sarah) Brenneman

4 cups fresh fruit in season (or canned fruit, thickened a little)
1/2 cup sugar (if using fresh fruit)
2 Tbsp. flour

Mix and let set while preparing batter.

Batter:

1 cup flour
1 cup sugar
1/4 tsp. salt
1 tsp. baking powder
1 egg

Beat egg and mix to dry ingredients to make a crumbly mixture. Put on top of fruit and bake till top is crisp and golden brown. Serve with milk for supper. Is good for people with high cholesterol since it has no shortening.

Oatmeal Brown Betty
Miss Mary U. Weaver

1/2 tsp. salt
1/2 tsp. baking soda
1 cup whole wheat flour
1/2 cup brown sugar
1 cup rolled oats
1/2 cup shortening (scant)
2 1/2 cups sliced apples
1/4 cup raisins

Mix dry ingredients; cut in shortening till mixture is crumbly. Spread half of crumbs in baking pan. Cover with apples and raisins. Put the remaining crumbs on top, covering the apples and raisins. Dot with butter. Drizzle 1/2 cup corn syrup or honey over top. Bake in moderate oven for 35 minutes, or until apples are soft. Serve with milk. Other fruit may be used.

Apple Crisp

6 apples, sliced
1 cup flour
1 cup sugar

1 tsp. baking powder
1 egg
$^3/_4$ tsp. salt

Put apples in bottom of pan. Mix the rest of ingredients and put on top of apples. Now pour $^1/_3$ cup cream over all and sprinkle with cinnamon. Bake; serve with milk.

Apple Pudding

2 cups apples, peeled and chopped
1 cup walnuts, chopped
1 cup flour
1 cup sugar
1 tsp. baking soda

$^1/_2$ tsp. salt
1 egg, beaten
3 Tbsp. melted butter
1 tsp. vanilla

Combine apples and nuts in bowl. Sift flour, sugar, baking soda, and salt together and blend with apple mixture. Combine egg, butter, and vanilla; mix well. Add to the rest and stir till moistened. Bake and serve plain or with milk or whipped cream. We like to eat this with milk for supper.

Pie Filling Crunch Dessert

$1^1/_2$ cups flour
$^3/_4$ cup rolled oats
1 cup brown sugar

$^1/_2$ tsp. baking soda
$^1/_2$ tsp. salt
$^1/_2$ cup softened oleo

Mix like pie dough crumbs. Put half of crumbs in 9x9" pan, then your favorite pie filling and the rest of crumbs. Serve warm with milk.

wooden spoon wisdom

Sin has so many tools,
but a lie is the handle which fits them all.

Cherry Rolly Polly

4 cups flour
4 tsp. baking powder
10 Tbsp. shortening

1 tsp. salt
1³/₄ cups milk
1³/₄ cups cherries

Make a sauce with:

2 cups cherry juice
2 cups water

1 cup sugar
2 Tbsp. cornstarch

Cook till thick; add 4 Tbsp. butter.

Mix flour, baking powder, and salt; cut in shortening. Add milk to make a dough. Roll dough ¹/₄" thick and spread with cherries. Roll up like a jelly roll. Cut in 1¹/₂" pieces and set in pans, then pour cherry sauce over top and bake. Serve with milk. Yum! Yum!

Apple Dumplings

2 cups flour
2¹/₂ tsp. baking powder
¹/₂ tsp. salt

²/₃ cup shortening
¹/₂ cup milk
6 apples, peeled and cut in halves

Sauce:

2 cups brown sugar
2 cups water

¹/₄ cup butter
¹/₂ tsp. cinnamon

Make dough like pie dough. Roll out dough; cut in squares. Place half an apple on each square. Wet edges of dough and press into a ball around the apple. Put dumplings in a pan; pour sauce over all and bake.

Rhubarb Delicious

1 cup flour
5 Tbsp. powdered sugar

¹/₂ cup butter or oleo
¹/₂ cup chopped nuts

Mix all ingredients and press into 9x9" pan. Bake 15 minutes at 350°. Beat 3 egg yolks; add 1¹/₄ cups sugar, ¹/₄ cup flour, ³/₄ Tbsp. salt, and 2 cups finely chopped rhubarb. Pour onto baked crust and bake 35–40 minutes more at 350°. Whip the egg whites; sweeten to taste. Spoon on top and return to oven until lightly browned.

Apple Cobbler

Miss Elsie Miller

Topping:

$^1/_2$ cup oleo spread, softened	1 cup flour
1 cup sugar	1 cup oatmeal
1 egg	$^3/_4$ tsp. cinnamon
1 tsp. vanilla	

Apple Filling:

8 lg. apples, peeled and sliced	$1^1/_2$ Tbsp. cornstarch
$^3/_4$ cup sugar	$1^1/_2$ tsp. cinnamon

Preheat oven to 350°. Cream oleo and sugar until creamy. Blend in egg and vanilla. Stir in flour, oatmeal, and cinnamon. In a separate bowl, combine apples, sugar, cornstarch, and cinnamon; mix well. Spread apple mixture into a shallow 3 qt. casserole dish. Spoon topping mixture evenly over apple filling. Bake 1 hour, or until golden brown. Serve warm. This is very good with ice cream.

Blackberry Cobbler

$^1/_4$ cup butter or margarine, softened	2 cups blackberries
$^1/_2$ cup sugar	$^3/_4$ cup raspberry or apple juice
1 cup flour	ice cream or whipped cream
2 tsp. baking powder	(optional)
$^1/_2$ cup milk	

In a mixing bowl, cream butter and sugar. Combine flour and baking powder; add to creamed mixture alternately with milk. Stir just until moistened. Pour into a greased $1^1/_2$ qt. baking pan. Sprinkle with blackberries. Pour juice over all. Bake at 350° for 45–50 minutes, or until golden brown. Serve warm; top with ice cream or whipped cream, if desired.

Shortcake

1 egg	1 tsp. baking powder
1 cup sugar	1 tsp. vanilla
$^1/_2$ cup milk	butter size of a walnut

Add enough flour to make a stiff cake batter. Bake at 350°.

Gingerbread

Mrs. Aden (Sarah) Miller

$1/2$ cup sugar	1 tsp. cinnamon
$1/2$ cup butter or lard	$1/2$ tsp. cloves
1 cup molasses	$1/2$ tsp. salt
1 egg, beaten	$1^1/2$ tsp. baking soda
$2^1/2$ cups flour	1 cup hot water
1 tsp. ginger	

Cream sugar and butter; add molasses, egg, and dry ingredients. Add baking soda and hot water. Bake at 325°–350° for 35 minutes.

Pineapple Cherry Crisp

Miss Elsie Miller

1 can pineapple rings	1 stick butter
1 can cherry pie filling	$3/4$ cup pecans
1 white cake mix	

Spread pineapple rings evenly in bottom of 13x9x2" pan. Pour cherry pie filling over pineapples. Sprinkle dry cake mix on top. Cut butter into slivers and dot on top of cake mix. Top with pecans. Bake at 350° for 45 minutes. Can be served warm or cold with ice cream.

Chocolate Sundae Pudding

Mrs. Wayne Hershberger

1 cup flour	2 tsp. baking powder
$3/4$ cup white sugar	2 Tbsp. cocoa

Sift together.

Add:

$1/2$ cup milk	1 tsp. vanilla

Put in pan and cover with the following sauce:

$1/2$ cup brown sugar	$1/2$ cup white sugar
1 cup boiling water	2 Tbsp. cocoa

Bake in moderate oven. This is good to serve warm with ice cream.

Hot Fudge Pudding

Miss Anna M. Miller

6 Tbsp. butter
$1^1/_2$ cups white sugar
1 cup milk
1 cup nuts (optional)

2 cups flour
2 tsp. baking powder
pinch of salt

Cream butter and sugar; add milk and nuts. Sift flour, baking powder, and salt. Mix all together and pour in ungreased cake pan. Mix 2 cups brown sugar and 2 Tbsp. cocoa; put on top of dough. Pour 2 cups boiling water over all. Serve with ice cream or whipped cream. Bake at 350°.

Baked Chocolate Fudge Pudding

Cream together:

3 Tbsp. shortening

$^3/_4$ cup white sugar

Sift together:

1 cup flour
$^1/_2$ tsp. salt

$1^1/_2$ tsp. baking powder

Add alternately with $^1/_2$ cup milk to creamed mixture. Fold in $^1/_2$ cup nuts or pecans. Put into ungreased pan. Mix 1 cup brown sugar, $^1/_4$ cup cocoa, and $^1/_4$ Tbsp. salt; sprinkle over top of batter. Do not stir. Pour $1^1/_4$ cups boiling water over top of batter and all. Bake at 350° for 40–45 minutes. Serve with ice cream, whipped cream, or milk.

Homemade Ice Cream

Mix:

3 cups sugar

6 Tbsp. flour

Add 3 cups milk and cook till thick; cool.

Add:

6 cups crushed peaches
3 ($^1/_2$ pt.) whipped cream

6 Tbsp. lemon juice

Ice Cream

Bring 1½ qts. milk to a boil. Soak 2 pkg. gelatin in 1 cup water. Mix 3 Tbsp. flour, 3 cups sugar, and 6 egg yolks with some milk. When cooked, add gelatin. Whip egg whites; add some Karo, vanilla, and a pinch of salt. For cracker pudding, add 2 Tbsp. cornstarch.

Ice Cream

1½ qts. milk, scalded	6 Tbsp. flour
2 cups white sugar	6 eggs, separated

Beat egg whites, adding 1 cup sugar gradually.

pinch of salt	1 pt. half & half or whipped
vanilla	topping

Snow Cream

In a large mixing bowl, beat 1 egg, 1 cup sugar, ⅔ cup evaporated milk, and 1 tsp. vanilla. Spoon in snow and beat till thick.

Ice Cream Pudding

¾ cup milk	1 sm. box instant pudding
1 pint ice cream, softened	

Mix milk and pudding; add ice cream. Beat with wire whisk till smooth. Sprinkle Oreo cookies or Ritz crackers on top.

Butterscotch Ice Cream Topping

1 cup light Karo	½ tsp. salt
1 cup brown sugar	3 tsp. butter
1 tsp. vanilla	½ cup milk

Cook together 5 minutes, stirring constantly. Store in cool place. Tastes like store-bought kind.

Snacks and Candy

When Christmastime
  Again rolls around,
Many girls and women
  In the kitchen will be found!

Making all kinds of goodies,
  Both candy and snacks.
Everywhere you look
  There are stacks and stacks!

There's mint patties, caramels,
  Peanut brittle, and fudge, too.
Bonbons and sugar plums,
  I've only named a few!

There's Muddy Buddies
  And granola bars,
Cracker Jack and party mix—
  Be sure and fill all your jars.

SNACKS AND CANDY MINI INDEX

wooden spoon wisdom

It's impossible to push yourself ahead by
patting yourself on the back.

Our Mailbox

My Dad has many original ideas. Like the air horn he's hooked up to his air tank. The air tank is used to provide air power for spray painting and finishing.

As you can see from my family's roadside mailbox, Dad is creative and likes painting!

Date Balls

Miss Sarah Brenneman

1 stick oleo

³/₄ cup sugar

2 egg yolks

1 cup chopped dates

Cook together until dates are soft.

Add:

pinch of salt

2 cups Rice Krispies

1 cup nuts

2 tsp. vanilla

Roll in balls and cover with coconut. Shape like cookies if desired.

Coconut Date Balls

Melt ¹/₂ cup butter. Add:

³/₄ cup granulated sugar

1 cup chopped dates

1 beaten eggs

1 Tbsp. milk

1 tsp. vanilla

¹/₄ tsp. salt

Bring first 3 ingredients to a good boil, while stirring. Add rest of ingredients. Cook 2 minutes, stirring. When cool (but not cold) add 2 cups Rice Krispies. Form in small balls; roll in coconut and chill.

Date Nut Candy

3 cups sugar

1 Tbsp. butter

1 cup milk

2 Tbsp. white syrup

1 cup nuts

1 cup dates

Mix sugar, butter, milk, and syrup. Cook till soft ball stage, then add nuts and dates and beat till stiff. Form in a roll and roll in waxed paper. Let cool till almost cold and cut ¹/₂" thick.

Date Roll Candy

Mrs. Aden (Sarah) Miller

Combine 2 cups sugar, 1 cup light Karo, and ¹/₂ tsp. salt. Cook until mixture reaches soft ball stage. Add 1 lb. chopped dates. Cook until mixture separates from pan when stirred. Add 1 cup chopped nuts, ¹/₂ cup shredded coconut, and ¹/₂ tsp. vanilla. Beat until cool. Pour on a wet towel and form a roll. Cut in slices.

Quick Caramels

1 can Eagle Brand milk	$^1/_2$ tsp. cream of tartar
1 lb. brown sugar	1 tsp. vanilla
1 cup white Karo	1 cup nuts
2 sticks butter	

Mix milk, sugar, Karo, and butter. Bring to a boil, stirring constantly. Boil 8–15 minutes, until soft ball forms in cold water and candy thermometer temperature is 238°. Blend in cream of tartar, vanilla, and nuts. Pour into small buttered cookie sheet. Cool, cut, and wrap each piece in plastic wrap.

Caramels

$^1/_2$ lb. butter or margarine	2 cups sugar
2 cups light corn syrup	$^1/_2$ cup sifted flour
2 - 15 oz. cans Eagle Brand milk	1 tsp. vanilla

In a heavy saucepan, melt butter; add corn syrup and sugar. Boil for 5 minutes over medium heat, stirring constantly. Add $1^1/_2$ cans Eagle Brand milk. Mix flour thoroughly with remaining milk, then add to corn syrup-sugar mixture. Boil until mixture darkens and forms a hard ball (240°). Stir constantly or mixture will stick. Add vanilla and pour into buttered pans. Allow to cool. Cut in 1" pieces with sharp, buttered knife. Wrap pieces in small squares of waxed paper.

Soft Pretzels

$2^1/_2$ cups lukewarm water	3 Tbsp. yeast
$^3/_4$ cup brown sugar	1 tsp. salt
7–8 cups flour	

Let stand and rise. Dip into soda water (2 Tbsp. baking soda to 1 cup water). Put on towel, then on greased cookie sheet and salt them. Bake at 450°. When baked, dip in melted butter.

Texas Bonbons

2 lbs. powdered sugar
1 - 15 oz. can sweetened condensed
  milk

$^1/_4$ cup melted butter
2 cups finely chopped pecans
$3^1/_2$ oz. flaked coconut

Mix together, using hands if necessary. Shape into balls smaller than walnuts. Let set 1 hour. Melt unsweetened chocolate with a little paraffin. Dip balls in chocolate and place on waxed paper. Makes about 11 dozen bonbons.

Coconut Bonbons

4 oz. cream cheese
$^1/_3$ cup butter
$2^1/_2$ cups coconut

$1^1/_2$ tsp. coconut flavor
$5^1/_2$ cups powdered sugar

Mix and form in balls and dip in chocolate.

Never Fail Fudge

1 lb. powdered sugar
$^1/_2$ cup milk

13 oz. peanut butter
7 oz. marshmallow creme

Mix milk and sugar in saucepan and bring to a boil. Let boil for 4 minutes. Take off heat and add peanut butter and marshmallow creme. Put in greased 13x9x2" pan.

Butterscotch Candy

Heat 1 cup white sugar and 1 cup light corn syrup till sugar is melted. Add 1 cup peanut butter and 6 cups Rice Krispies; press in buttered pan.

Frosting:
Melt 6 oz. chocolate chips and 6 oz. butterscotch chips in double boiler. Do not let water boil. Spread on Rice Krispies mixture.

Buttery Peanut Brittle

2 cups sugar	1 cup butter or margarine
1 cup light corn syrup	2 cups peanuts
$^1/_2$ cup water	1 tsp. baking soda

Combine sugar, corn syrup, and water in 3 qt. saucepan. Cook and stir until sugar dissolves. When syrup boils, blend in butter. Stir frequently after mixture reaches 230° on candy thermometer. Add nuts when temperature reaches 280° and stir constantly until temperature reaches hard crack stage (305°). Remove from heat; quickly stir in baking soda, mixing thoroughly. Pour onto 2 well-buttered cookie sheets. Spread as thin as possible with spoon. Let cool. Loosen from pans and break into pieces. Makes $2^1/_2$ lbs.

Sugar Plums

$^1/_2$ cup butter or oleo	2 eggs, slightly beaten
1 cup white sugar	

Put in pan on medium heat; stir. Add $1^1/_4$ cups chopped dates. Cook, stirring constantly, for 5 minutes, then add $^1/_4$ cup flour. Keep stirring and cook 7 minutes more. Remove from heat.

Add:

1 tsp. vanilla	$^1/_4$ tsp. salt
1 cup chopped nuts	

Mix well; cool enough to handle. Form into plum-sized balls and roll in red sugar. Decorate with green leaves made with icing.

Hard Candy

$3^3/_4$ cups white sugar	1 tsp. desired flavoring
$1^1/_2$ cups light Karo	1 tsp. desired coloring
1 cup water	

Sprinkle 18x24" strip of heavy-duty aluminum foil with powdered sugar. Mix first 3 ingredients in heavy saucepan. Stir over medium heat until sugar dissolves. Boil, without stirring, until temperature reaches 310°, or until drops of syrup form hard and brittle threads in cold water. Remove from heat. Stir in flavoring and coloring. Pour onto foil. Break into pieces. Store in airtight container.

Valley Taffy

4 cups sugar

2 cups cream and milk

2 cups light Karo

paraffin the size of a walnut

1 Tbsp. Knox gelatine, soaked in

2 cups water

Mix all together, except gelatine, and cook 15 minutes. Add gelatine and cook until it forms a hard ball in cold water. Better yet, use a candy thermometer; boil to hard boil. Pour into well-buttered pans.

miriam's memories

One day Mom and we children decided to go and spend the day at Grandpas. We hitched Lassie, the horse, to the buggy and started for Grandpas. When we wanted to make the last turn before Grandpas' lane, Lassie fell down flat. Mom quickly got out with Baby Reuben. Just then Lassie jumped up and started running. Mom yelled, "Grab the reins!" I got them and started pulling as hard as I could. I was only eight years old, so it probably wasn't too hard. Lassie kept running and we were almost at Grandpas' lane. Aaron, then six, was sitting in the back of the buggy. He reached forward and helped me pull on the reins. Sarah and Marvin, who were also sitting in the back, sat there grinning, not knowing what danger they were in. Just as we got to Grandpa's lane Lassie stopped. No one was hurt and we arrived at Grandpas safe and sound and very thankful!

Mint Patties

1 lb. powdered sugar
2 tsp. cream
1 Tbsp. soft butter
1 egg white (unbeaten)
1 tsp. vanilla

Mix together and shape into patties. Dip in chocolate.

Peanut Butter Balls

2 cups peanut butter
2 tsp. salt
$^3/_4$ stick butter or oleo
1 lb. powdered sugar

Mix; form into balls. Roll in melted chocolate.

Potato Candy

Cook 2 potatoes, the size of an egg; mash and work in powdered sugar, just enough to make stiff. Roll thin; spread with peanut butter. Roll like jelly roll, then slice.

Muddy Buddies (Snacks)

9 cups Chex cereal (Corn, Rice, or Wheat)
1 cup semi-sweet chocolate chips
$^1/_2$ cup peanut butter
$^1/_4$ cup butter
1 tsp. vanilla
$1^1/_2$ cups powdered sugar

Pour cereal into large bowl; set aside. In small saucepan, over low heat, melt chocolate chips, peanut butter, and butter until smooth, stirring often. Remove from heat; stir in vanilla. Pour chocolate mixture over cereal, stirring until all pieces are evenly coated. Pour cereal mixture into a large plastic bag with powdered sugar. Seal securely and shake until all pieces are well coated. Spread on waxed paper to cool.

Crunchies

1 cup butterscotch chips
$^1/_4$ cup peanut butter
$3^1/_2$–4 cups corn flakes

Melt butterscotch chips in top of double boiler; stir in peanut butter. Pour over corn flakes and mix well. Drop by teaspoonfuls onto waxed paper. Cool.

Crunchy Treat

3 lbs. chocolate
2 lbs. butterscotch coating
2 cups peanut butter
1 box Rice Krispies

Melt chocolate, butterscotch, and peanut butter. Pour over Rice Krispies and mix well. Press in pan and cut into squares.

Clark Bar Candy

1 cup butter
1 lb. crunchy peanut butter
$2^1/_2$ cups powdered sugar
1 lb. graham crackers, crushed
3 tsp. vanilla

Mix ingredients with hand. Roll in balls and dip in chocolate.

Granola Bars

$^1/_4$ cup margarine
10 oz. marshmallows
$^1/_2$ cup peanut butter
5 cups Rice Krispies
1 cup quick oats
1 cup chocolate chips

Melt margarine; add marshmallows and peanut butter. Stir over low heat until melted. Add Rice Krispies and oatmeal; stir until coated. Add chocolate chips and mix well. Press mixture into 10x15" pan. Cool and cut into bars.

Mounds Bars

$1^1/_2$ cups graham cracker crumbs
$^1/_3$ cup butter, melted
$^1/_3$ cup sugar
2 cups coconut
14 oz. sweetened condensed milk
1 cup chocolate chips
2 Tbsp. peanut butter

Combine cracker crumbs, butter, and sugar. Press into bottom of 10x11" pan. Combine coconut and milk; spread over crust. Bake at 375° for 15 minutes. Melt chocolate chips and peanut butter together and spread over warm crust. Cool; cut into bars.

Crunch Bars

1/2 cup butter or margarine	1 1/3 cups coconut
3 cups bite-sized rice or wheat cereal squares, crushed	14 oz. sweetened condensed milk
1 cup butterscotch or peanut butter chips	1 cup chopped pecans
	2 cups additional cereal (uncrushed)

Melt butter in 13x9x2" pan. Sprinkle rest of ingredients over butter in order given. Press down firmly. Bake at 350° for 25–30 minutes. Cool thoroughly before cutting into bars.

Indoor S'mores

In 3 qt. saucepan, combine:

2 Tbsp. margarine	11 oz. chocolate chips
2/3 cup light corn syrup	

Heat to boiling, stirring constantly. Remove from heat and stir in 1 tsp. vanilla. Pour chocolate over 10 oz. Golden Grahams cereal. Toss quickly to coat completely. Fold in 3 cups miniature marshmallows. Press into buttered 13x9x2" pan. Let stand at least 2 hours before cutting into squares.

Rice Krispie Candy

40 large marshmallows	5 cups Rice Krispies
1/4 cup butter	M&Ms (if desired)

Melt butter and marshmallows in top of double boiler. Pour over Rice Krispies in bowl; mix well. If desired, add M&Ms. Pour into buttered pan and press down with spoon. Cut into squares.

Rescue Rangers Bars

1/4 cup margarine, melted	2 cups corn flakes
1/4 cup sugar	1 cup coarsely chopped peanuts
1/4 cup honey	1/4 cup raisins

Measure margarine, sugar, and honey in a saucepan. Stir until smooth. Boil a few minutes. Add corn flakes, peanuts, and raisins. Press mixture evenly into a 9x9x2" pan.

Rocky Road Squares
Mrs. Aden (Sarah) Miller

3 lbs. milk chocolate
1/2 lb. soft butter

3 lb. walnuts, broken
10 oz. miniature marshmallows

Melt chocolate; stir till smooth. Add butter and mix well (will be thick, but warm). Set in cold place until it thickens around edges. Stir occasionally while cooling. Bring into warm room and stir 5–10 minutes, until creamy and thinner. Add marshmallows and walnuts. Pour in waxed paper-lined cookie sheet. Press 3/4" thick and cool. Cut into squares at room temperature.

miriam's memories

Dad remembers when his family and two other families got together to make a huge batch of Cracker Jack. After it was made they greased a long table and spread Cracker Jack on it. Then came the fun part! They would all sit around the table and try to eat a path through all the way across the table. After they were done eating they divided it so each family got some to take along home.

When Dad was a little boy, he saw the Cracker Jack can standing there. It was a tall can and just a little Cracker Jack was left over. He reached in a bit too far and fell in head-first. The rest of the family was out in the barn milking so he had to wait until they came in to get him out. I think he got all the Cracker Jack he wanted that evening.

Cracker Jack

1 lb. butter
5 lbs. white sugar

1/2 gal. light Karo
coloring

Boil this to soft crack stage, then add 1 tsp. cream of tartar. Boil to hard crack stage. Pour over 7–8 gallons popcorn and 1 lb. raw peanuts.

Baked Caramel Corn

6 qt. popped popcorn
1 cup butter or margarine
2 cups packed brown sugar
$^1/_2$ cup corn syrup

1 tsp. salt
$^1/_2$ tsp. baking soda
1 tsp. vanilla

Preheat oven to 250°. Pour popcorn in a greased roasting pan. In a saucepan, slowly melt butter; stir in brown sugar, corn syrup, and salt. Bring to a boil, stirring constantly. Boil, without stirring, for 5 minutes. Remove from heat; stir in baking soda and vanilla. Gradually pour over popcorn, mixing well. Bake 1 hour, stirring every 15 minutes. Remove from oven; cool completely. Break apart. Makes 6 qts.

Kool-Aid Popcorn Balls

9 cups popped popcorn
1 cup sugar

1 cup light corn syrup
1 env. Kool-Aid (any flavor)

Place popcorn in a large, lightly buttered bowl. Bring syrup, sugar, and Kool-Aid to a boil in a saucepan; boil over medium heat until mixture will separate into a hard thread when dropped into very cold water, about 6–7 minutes. Remove from heat and pour over popcorn, mixing quickly to coat well. Let stand 3 minutes. Shape into 1$^1/_2$" balls. Makes about 3 dozen.

Party Mix

pretzels
Cheerios
Fruit Dots cereal
3 Tbsp. Worcestershire sauce

Honeycomb cereal
cheddar-flavored crackers
1 lb. butter

This makes a 3 qt. mixing bowl almost full.

Finger Jell-O

4 sm. boxes Jell-O
3 pkg. Knox gelatine

4 cups hot water
$^1/_2$ cup cold water

Mix Jell-O and hot water. Mix gelatine and cold water. Let stand a few minutes, then add to Jell-O. Pour into pans. Cut into squares when cold.

Cheese Ball

1 lb. Velveeta cheese
1 - 8 oz. pkg. cream cheese
3/4 cup Cheez Whiz
1/2 cup cheddar cheese
3 oz. dried beef, chopped very fine

3 Tbsp. Miracle Whip
1 tsp. Worcestershire sauce
1/4 tsp. onion salt
walnuts, chopped fine (optional)

Let cheese soften at room temperature. Mix all ingredients with cheese until blended. Form into ball and cover with chopped nuts, if desired. Refrigerate until ready to serve.

Fudge Puddles

1/2 cup butter or margarine, softened
1/2 cup creamy peanut butter
1/2 cup sugar
1/2 cup packed light brown sugar
1 egg

1/2 tsp. vanilla
1 1/4 cups all-purpose flour
3/4 tsp. baking soda
1/2 tsp. salt

Fudge Filling:

1 cup milk chocolate chips
1 cup semi-sweet chocolate chips

1 cup sweetened condensed milk
1 tsp. vanilla extract

In a bowl, cream butter, sugar, peanut butter, egg, and vanilla. Add flour, soda, and salt; mix well. Shape into 48 balls. Place in lightly greased mini muffin tins. Bake at 325° for 14–16 minutes. Remove from oven and immediately make wells with melon baller. Cool in pans 5 minutes before removing. Melt filling in double boiler over simmering water. Fill each shell; sprinkle with nuts.

Crackers to Snack

1 stick oleo

3/4 cup brown sugar

Cook a few minutes. Pour over 24 soda crackers. Bake in 375° oven for 5 minutes. Take out; put chocolate chips and nuts on top. Put back in oven for a few minutes.

Miscellaneous

When canning season
  Is in full swing,
Lots and lots of work
  It will bring!

There's lots of stuff to can,
  Including blackberry,
Tomatoes, meat, fruit,
  And vegetables it will be!

Canning makes everyone
  Tired, hot, and grumpy.
But think of all the times
  You'll open a jar when you're
    hungry!

When busy summer is over
  And it's fall,
Look at all those full jars
  And be thankful for them all!

MISCELLANEOUS MINI INDEX

MISCELLANEOUS MINI INDEX

The Wishing Well

*L*ong summer days. Hard work. Hours of play. What is more refreshing than a cool drink from the well?

Nowadays they call it a wishing well. I don't know, but I think it's because young girls like me used to dawdle over the edge—some into the water—and dream of good things to come. In summer I long for the cold of winter. In winter I can't believe there is such a thing as a barefoot day.

Young girls like myself dream of a home of our own. A husband to love. A family to care for. Won't it be something to look out my own kitchen window and see my daughter at the wishing well? That's a long way off . . . but, oh, well, I need to get back to shelling peas on the back porch. Dad's coming home soon and Mom needs help with dinner. Good-bye for now.

Mixed Hamburger to Can

15 lbs. hamburger
1 cup oatmeal
7 slices bread crumbs
3 cups water

$^1/_2$ cup salt
36 crackers, crushed
pepper to taste

Makes 9 qts.

To Can Fish

Soak meat in salt water 1 hour (first remove skin—bones do not need to be removed). Cut into 1" chunks. Pack in pint jars. Add 1 tsp. lemon juice. Put in pressure cooker for 100 minutes at 14 lbs. pressure.

Homemade Bologna

25 lbs. hamburger
$^3/_4$ lb. Tender Quick
1 qt. warm water
1 Tbsp. pepper
1 handful seasoning salt

$^1/_2$ cup sugar
1 tsp. garlic
1 tsp. Liquid Smoke
1 qt. warm water

Mix first 3 ingredients and let stand overnight. Next morning, add rest of ingredients. Mix all together and cold pack 2 hours.

How to Can Steaks

1 gal. water
2 cups salt

2 cups sugar

Dissolve and divide into 14 quart jars, then fill with steaks. Cold pack 1 hour.

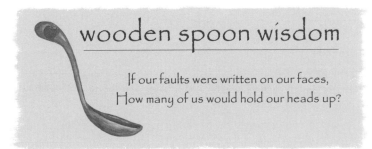

wooden spoon wisdom

If our faults were written on our faces,
How many of us would hold our heads up?

Canning Meat Loaf
Mrs. Melvin (Esther) Miller

20 lbs. hamburger
5 eggs
45 crackers
8 cups water
1 Tbsp. Lawry's seasoning salt

4 oz. salt
5 slices bread
1 1/2 cups oatmeal
1 1/2 tsp. pepper

Mix and press into jars. Pressure cook 1 hour.

Brine for Smoking
Mrs. Paul (Esther) Hochstetler

1/2 gal. water
2/3 cup salt
1 cup brown sugar
1 1/2 tsp. black pepper
1/2 tsp. ground cloves
3/4 tsp. white pepper

1 tsp. onion powder
1 tsp. garlic powder
2 1/2 oz. Liquid Smoke
1/8 tsp. crushed hot peppers
   (if desired)

Mix together; heat to boiling. Cool. Soak meat in brine 1 or 2 days and inject some of the brine with a needle if pieces of meat are big. Smoke to taste. This is very good even if you don't want to smoke it. It makes the meat really juicy. Especially good for turkey.

Strawberries to Can

3 qts. strawberries, chopped slightly   1 box Danish dessert
3 cups white sugar

Mix together and put in jars. Cold pack 7 minutes.

Red Beets

1 cup vinegar
1 qt. sugar
1 qt. beet water

1 tsp. whole cloves
2 sticks cinnamon
1 Tbsp. salt

Cook and peel beets. Cut into 1" pieces. Put in jars. Put all syrup ingredients in saucepan and bring to a boil. Pour over beets. Cold pack 1/2 hour. This makes enough syrup for 4 qts. beets.

Pizza Sauce

1 cup onions
2 Tbsp. Wesson oil
3 qt. tomato juice
2 cups brown sugar
1 tsp. salt

dash of pepper
$^3/_4$ tsp. garlic salt
$^3/_4$ tsp. oregano
$^3/_4$ tsp. chili powder

Brown onions in oil and add the rest. Thicken with 4 Tbsp. clear jel. Bring to a boil and simmer 20 minutes. Put in jars, boiling hot, and seal.

Canned Pepper

2 qts. white vinegar
1 qt. water
2 cups sugar

1 Tbsp. salt
corn oil

Cut peppers in pieces and pack in canning jars. Combine vinegar, water, sugar, and salt. Boil a few minutes, then add 1 Tbsp. oil to each quart of peppers. Pour vinegar mixture over top and seal immediately. These are nice and crisp. Good on pizza or in salads.

Sweet Corn to Can

Fill quart jars with corn loosely (do not pack).
To each jar, add:

1 Tbsp. lemon juice or ReaLemon   1 tsp. salt
1 tsp. sugar

Fill with water as usual. Cook in pressure cooker at 10 lbs. pressure for 15 minutes.

Stained Dish Solution

$^1/_2$ cup bleach
1 can lye

1 cup Tide or other detergent

Dissolve lye in cold water, then add rest of ingredients. Fill canner $^3/_4$ full with hot water. Works best if water is almost boiling. Put dishes in for 5 minutes, or until clean. Use handy tong to pull them out. Do not put your hands in.

Pork 'n' Beans (to can)

Mrs. Ivan A. Miller

8 lbs. dry navy beans (long Northern)	3 cups white sugar
5 lbs. ham, cut up fine	4 cups brown sugar
$1/8$ cup salt	$1^{1}/_{2}$ - 26 oz. bottles ketchup
4 qt. tomato juice	$1/2$ tsp. red pepper
1 lg. onion, cut up fine	1 tsp. dry mustard
3 cups water	1 tsp. cinnamon

Soak beans overnight, then cook till tender. Pour off water. Add the other ingredients (fry onions and ham before adding). Add grease and all (bacon may be used instead of ham). Cold pack 3 hours. One batch makes 15 qts.

Corn Salad

12 ears of corn	2 qts. vinegar
3 bunches celery	2 Tbsp. celery seed
1 head cabbage	3 cups sugar

Cook corn on cobs for 5 minutes. Cut off corn. Mix all together and boil 15 minutes. Put in cans and seal.

Mixed Pickle

8 cups sliced cucumber	1 tsp. turmeric
4 green peppers	2 cups vinegar
2 cups sliced onions	1 tsp. celery seed
$3/4$ cup cooked carrots (more if desired)	1 stick cinnamon
celery	2–3 cups sugar
cauliflower	salt (if needed)

Boil vegetables and vinegar mixture together for 20 minutes. Put in jars and seal while hot.

Cheez Whiz

Miss Leanna Miller

3 lbs. Velveeta cheese	$1^{3}/_{4}$ cups milk
1 can Milnot	

Mix together and melt over low heat. Put in jars and cold pack 15 minutes.

Ketchup

1 peck tomatoes	3 Tbsp. salt
3 lg. onions	4 cups sugar
1 pt. vinegar	$^1/_2$ oz. ketchup spice

Cook tomatoes and onions till soft. Put through strainer, then drain in jelly bag (throw away juice). Bring to a boil, then add rest of ingredients. Boil 10 minutes, then seal in jars.

Substitute for ketchup spice:

$^1/_2$ tsp. cloves	$^1/_2$ tsp. dry mustard
$^1/_2$ tsp. cinnamon	

Sandwich Spread

3–4 green tomatoes	2 lg. stalks of celery
12 lg. peppers	1 qt. onions

Measure all this, then grind and add 1 cup salt. Drain overnight in a cloth bag. Press remaining juice in the morning. Add 1 qt. vinegar and $1^1/_2$ qts. sugar and boil for 25–30 minutes. When cold, add 1 qt. mayonnaise (more if desired) and $^1/_2$ small jar mustard.

Sandwich Spread
Mrs. Simon J. Brenneman

12 green peppers	12 green tomatoes
12 red peppers	6 onions
12 yellow peppers	

Grind all these together.

Add:

1 pt. mustard	1 tsp. celery seed
3 cups sugar	1 Tbsp. salt
1 pt. vinegar	1 cup flour

Cook 10–15 minutes.

Add:

1 qt. salad dressing	1 lb. Velveeta cheese

Reheat and seal in jars, but keep stirred while cooking!

Sandwich Spread

Mrs. Wm. (Laura) Miller

12 green tomatoes   2 onions
12 green peppers

Grind together, then drain.

2 cups prepared mustard   1 Tbsp. salt
6 cups sugar   1 Tbsp. celery salt
2 cups vinegar

Bring last part to a boil; add ground mixture. Boil 15–20 minutes. Add 1 cup flour by making a slightly thick paste with water and vinegar. Bring back to a boil; take from stove and add 1 qt. salad dressing. Can quickly. One batch yields 9–10 pints.

Hamburger Pickle Recipe

Put 1 gallon sliced pickles in salt brine made of 1 gallon water and 1 cup salt. Let stand for 3 days. Drain off and wash in clear water. Boil pickles in water to cover and 1 Tbsp. alum (or more) for 10 minutes. Drain off. Make a syrup of 2 cups vinegar, 2 cups water, 3 lbs. sugar, 1 Tbsp. allspice, and 1 Tbsp. celery seed. Put spice in a bag and cook till clear and glossy.

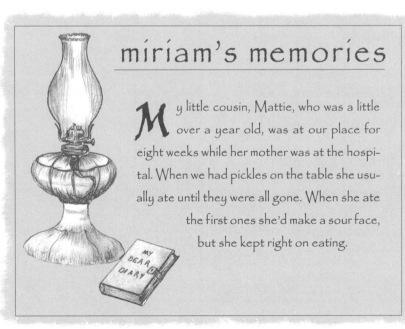

miriam's memories

My little cousin, Mattie, who was a little over a year old, was at our place for eight weeks while her mother was at the hospital. When we had pickles on the table she usually ate until they were all gone. When she ate the first ones she'd make a sour face, but she kept right on eating.

Pickles

1 gallon sliced pickles
2 cups sliced onions
6 cups sugar
3 tsp. mustard seed

3 tsp. celery seed
1 tsp. turmeric
3 cups vinegar
$^1/_2$ Tbsp. salt

Heat all together and put in jars. Makes 8 pints.

Bread and Butter Pickles

1 gallon cucumbers, sliced
4 onions, sliced

$^1/_2$ cup salt

Put together; let stand 3 hours, then drain. Add:

4 cups sugar
3 cups vinegar
1 Tbsp. celery seed

1 Tbsp. dry mustard
$^1/_2$ Tbsp. turmeric powder

Pour this mixture over pickles. Put on low heat. Bring to a boil.

Refrigerator Pickles

6 cups sliced cucumbers
1 cup sliced green pepper
1 cup sliced onions
1 tsp. celery seed

2 Tbsp. salt
1 cup vinegar
2 cups white sugar

Mix all together and store in refrigerator. Ready to eat in 24 hours.

Dill Pickles

1 tsp. salt

$^1/_2$ tsp. dill seed

Put pickle slices in jars which have 3 slices onions in bottom. Put dill and salt in on top. Mix $^1/_2$ cup white sugar and $^1/_2$ cup vinegar and some water. Put over pickles in jars. Cold pack, bringing just to boiling point, then remove from heat. This is for 1 pint.

Banana Pickles

Mrs. John (Sarah) Brenneman

2 cups sugar
2 cups water
1 cup vinegar
1 Tbsp. dry mustard
1 tsp. celery seed
1 tsp. turmeric
1 Tbsp. salt

Peel and slice pickles lengthwise and pack in jars. Pour brine over pickles and cold pack to a good boil.

Canning Pickles

Mrs. Aden (Sarah) Miller

4 qts. pickles
1/2 qt. onions
2 cups sugar
4 tsp. salt
1 Tbsp. celery seed
1/2 tsp. dry mustard
1/2 tsp. turmeric
1 qt. vinegar

Mix and bring to a boiling point. Put in cans.

Onion Dill Pickles

Miss Laura Weaver

1 1/2 cups vinegar
3 cups water
3 cups sugar
2 Tbsp. salt
onions
dill heads

Slice pickles and fill to neck of can. Add 1 onion slice and 1 head of dill to each can. Heat other ingredients and fill cans. Put hot water in canner and cold pack only till boiling. Makes 4 qts.

Seven Day Sweet Pickles

Cover 7 lbs. medium pickles with boiling water. Let stand 24 hours. Repeat this for 4 days, fresh water each time. On fifth day, cut pickles in chunks. Now take 1 qt. vinegar, 8 cups sugar, 2 Tbsp. salt, and 2 Tbsp. mixed pickle spice. Boil this together and pour over pickles. Let stand 24 hours. Drain and boil again; pour over pickles. Let stand 24 hours. The seventh day, drain off again and bring to a boil; add cucumbers and bring to a boil. Put in cans and seal.

Cucumber Cinnamon Rings

2 gal. lg. cucumber rings, peeled
  and seeds removed

2 cups lime
8½ qt. water

Let stand 24 hours. Drain and wash in clear water. Soak 3 hours in cold water, then drain off. Simmer 2 hours in 1 cup vinegar, 1 Tbsp. alum, 1 bottle red food coloring, and water to cover. Drain off.

Make syrup of:
  2 cups vinegar
  2 cups water

10 cups sugar

Pour over rings and let stand overnight. Drain and reheat 3 days. The last day, heat and add 1 pkg. cinnamon red hots. Pack in jars and seal.

Sweet Dill Pickles

2 cups vinegar
2 cups sugar
2 cups water

2 Tbsp. salt
pickles
dill

Slice pickles into jars. Place a sprig of dill (or dill seed) on top of pickles in each jar. Heat the rest of ingredients and pour over pickles in jars. This should be enough syrup for 8 quarts. Cold pack 5 minutes.

Mint Jelly

5 cups boiling water
5 cups firmly packed mint leaves
½ cup lemon juice
6 cups sugar

1 - 1¾ oz. pkg. powdered fruit
  pectin
green food coloring

In a large bowl, pour water over mint leaves and let set for 1 hour. Press juice from leaves; measure 5 cups and pour into large saucepan. Add lemon juice, sugar, and pectin; stir well. Bring to a rolling boil. Boil hard for 1 minute, stirring constantly. Remove from heat; skim off any foam. Add a few drops of green food coloring.

Cold Sugar Spread

1/2 gal. white Karo
6 cups brown sugar
1 qt. marshmallow topping
1 tsp. maple flavor

Mix all together.

Peanut Butter Spread

1 lb. peanut butter
1 qt. light Karo
2 cups pancake syrup
1 cup marshmallow topping

Mix all together. If it is too thick, add warm water to make it the right consistency.

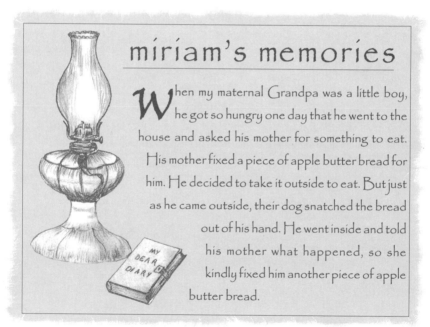

miriam's memories

When my maternal Grandpa was a little boy, he got so hungry one day that he went to the house and asked his mother for something to eat. His mother fixed a piece of apple butter bread for him. He decided to take it outside to eat. But just as he came outside, their dog snatched the bread out of his hand. He went inside and told his mother what happened, so she kindly fixed him another piece of apple butter bread.

Apple Butter

2 gal. apples
2 lbs. sugar
1 qt. dark Karo
1 qt. light Karo

Cook 3 hours. Do not open or stir while cooking. Put through strainer. Add cinnamon and cloves; bring to a boil. Put in jars and seal.

Elderberry Preserves (Hulla Malosich)

1/2 gal. Karo
1/2 gal. white sugar

1 pt. elderberry juice

Cook together 10 minutes. Put in jars and seal. Use a big kettle so it won't boil over.

Beet Jelly

Miss Barbara Miller

2 1/3 cups beet juice
1/3 cup lemon juice
1 pkg. Sure Jell

4 1/2 cups sugar
1/3 cup raspberry Jell-O

Mix beet juice, lemon juice, and Sure Jell; bring to a boil. Add sugar; stir well and bring to a full rolling boil for 5 minutes. Add Jell-O. Put in jars and seal. Use a big saucepan so it won't boil over.

Pineapple Preserves

1 qt. crushed pineapple
1 qt. light Karo

5 lbs. white sugar

Cook 5 minutes.

Egg in a Nest

1 slice bread
1 egg
1 Tbsp. butter

salt
pepper

Cut a 2" square hole in the bread slice. Melt butter in skillet. Put bread in skillet and break egg into the hole. When halfway done, flip to fry other side. Have a soft yolk. Toast the cut-out piece of bread and use to dunk.

Peanut Butter and Jam Sandwiches

Spread a piece of bread with peanut butter. Spread another piece of bread with strawberry jam. Put them together and eat it! It's good!

Quick and Easy Sandwiches

Miss Sara Miller

1½ lbs. hamburger
1 sm. onion, diced

1 sm. box Velveeta cheese
1 can cream of mushroom soup

Brown hamburger and onion in a little butter. When fried, add soup and cheese which has been cut. Stir until melted. Serve hot on buns.

Sandwich Filling

1 qt. meat (cut up chicken or
fried hamburger)
1 qt. canned pickles
10 eggs, hard boiled and grated

½ cup white sugar
salt and pepper to taste
2 cups salad dressing (or more)

Add more or less of each ingredient to suit your taste. Add enough salad dressing to make it the consistency you want. Stir everything together. Put on bread to eat. Delicious cold sandwiches.

miriam's memories

One Sunday evening we were making peanut butter and jam sandwiches for a quick supper. We had the bread spread with peanut butter all in a row on the table. Little Laura, who was eighteen months old and knew better, climbed on the table. One of the older ones wanted to pull her off the table and she fell facedown on a piece of peanut butter bread. Her WHOLE face was covered with peanut butter. We all started laughing and everyone had to come look at her. After we were done laughing someone looked at the bread and there was a small dent where her little nose had hit so we started laughing all over again.

Peanut Butter and Jelly French Toast

12 slices bread	3/4 cup milk
3/4 cup peanut butter	1/4 tsp. salt
6 Tbsp. jelly or jam	2 Tbsp. butter or margarine
3 eggs	

Spread peanut butter on 6 slices of bread; spread jelly on other 6 slices of bread. Put one slice of each together to form sandwiches. In a mixing bowl, lightly beat eggs; add milk and salt and mix together. Melt butter in a large skillet over medium heat. Dip sandwiches in egg mixture, coating well. Place in skillet and brown both sides. Serve immediately.

Chicken on the Grill   *Ivan Miller*

2 Tbsp. seasoned salt	1 tsp. black pepper
2 Tbsp. garlic salt	1 tsp. salt
2 Tbsp. Accent	

Mix together and sprinkle both sides of chicken. For full flavor, marinate for 4 hours. Chicken leg quarters take approximately 25 minutes; drumsticks 20 minutes. This is also good on pork chops. Takes 7 minutes on each side over a hot fire.

Fish on the Grill   *Ivan Miller*

Wrap each piece of fish in tinfoil with butter and a slice of onion; sprinkle fish with ReaLemon.

Potatoes on the Grill   *Ivan Miller*

8 unpeeled potatoes	1 cup (4 oz.) shredded cheddar
1 Tbsp. butter	or mozzarella cheese
salt and pepper to taste	

Slice potatoes like thick French fries. Place on a large piece of aluminum foil. Add butter, salt and pepper. Seal foil. Grill till potatoes are tender, then sprinkle with cheese and reseal foil until cheese melts. Makes 8–10 servings.

Flannel Pancakes

2 cups flour
2 Tbsp. sugar
1 Tbsp. melted butter
4 tsp. baking powder

1 egg
salt
enough milk to make a thin
   batter

Mix all together and fry in oil.

Amish Cereal

12 cups rolled oats
6 cups coconut
6 cups wheat germ

3 cups sugar
3 tsp. salt
1 cup vegetable oil or oleo

Mix all together and toast at 300° till golden brown.

Favorite Granola

Miss Laura Weaver

12 cups quick oats
8 cups Rice Krispies
2 cups brown sugar
2 tsp. salt

$1/2$ cup vegetable oil or butter
coconut, raisins, or chocolate
   chips (can be added)

Toast for 1 hour at 300°. Have a syrup ready of 1 cup honey and $1/2$ cup butter. Slowly drizzle over top of cereal; toss lightly and continue to toast for $1/2$ hour. Take out of oven and add coconut, chips, or raisins.

Cereal

8 cups rolled oats
$1^1/2$ cups brown sugar
1 pkg. graham crackers
2 cups butter, melted

4 cups wheat flour
1 Tbsp. baking soda
1 Tbsp. salt
nuts

Mix all together, put in pans, and toast 1 hour at 250°. When almost cooled, add butterscotch chips.

Good Grape-Nuts

7 cups wheat flour
3 cups brown sugar
4 cups sour milk
2 tsp. baking soda

2 tsp. salt
$1/2$ cup melted oleo
2 tsp. vanilla

Bake as a loaf cake. Crumble or rub through a screen and toast.

Orange Butter Frosting

$1/4$ cup butter or margarine
$1/4$ cup orange juice

3 cups powdered sugar
$1/2$ tsp. grated orange peel

Chocolate-Cinnamon Frosting

6 Tbsp. butter or oleo, softened
$2^2/3$ cups powdered sugar
$1/3$ cup milk

$1/2$ cup cocoa
$1-1^1/2$ tsp. cinnamon

Creamy Chocolate Frosting

1 lb. powdered sugar
1 stick margarine, softened
3 Tbsp. cocoa

1 tsp. vanilla
$4^1/2$ Tbsp. milk

Marshmallow Creme Filling

$1/2$ cup white shortening
2 cups powdered sugar

1 cup marshmallow creme
vanilla

Add enough cream to spread. This is good to spead between layer cakes, jelly rolls, or cookies.

Creamy White Frosting

1/2 cup shortening
1/2 cup butter or oleo
1 tsp. vanilla extract

1 tsp. almond extract
4 cups powdered sugar
3–4 Tbsp. milk

Creamy Nut Filling

3/4 cup sugar
3 Tbsp. flour
3/4 cup cream
1/2 tsp. salt

3 Tbsp. butter or margarine
3/4 cup chopped pecans, toasted
1 tsp. vanilla

Combine sugar, flour, cream, salt, and butter in a saucepan. Cook over medium heat until thickened. Stir in pecans and vanilla. Cool.

Ruthe's Favorite Frosting

3 heaping Tbsp. creamy peanut
    butter
3 heaping Tbsp. butter, softened
1 tsp. vanilla
2 cups powdered sugar

3 heaping Tbsp. cocoa
1/8 tsp. salt
2–4 Tbsp. milk (more, as needed)

Mix together peanut butter, butter, and vanilla. Stir in powdered sugar, cocoa, and salt. Add milk, stirring until you reach the desired consistency.

Glazed Donuts   *Mrs. Henry (Esther) Miller*

5 cups scalded milk
7 1/2 cups flour
5 pkgs. dry yeast
5 eggs, beaten

1 1/4 cups sugar
10 cups flour
1 1/4 cups lard
5 tsp. salt

Glaze:

1 pkg. gelatin, soaked in 1/4 cup
    cold water
1 box powdered sugar

2 Tbsp. melted butter
1/4 cup boiling water
1 tsp. vanilla

Beat first 3 ingredients and let rise till double in size. Add rest of ingredients. Roll out and let rise. Fry in hot vegetable oil. Glaze while donuts are still warm.

Donuts

Miss Katie Miller

10 lbs. donut mix
4 cups bread flour

10 cups warm water
8 Tbsp. yeast

Glaze:

1 lb. powdered sugar
6 Tbsp. hot water
1 Tbsp. vanilla

1 Tbsp. cornstarch
$1/2$ Tbsp. melted butter

Donuts: Let donuts rise until about double in size.

Glaze: Put in boiling water till right thickness.

Hot Chocolate Mix

Miss Alma Hershberger

2 lbs. dry milk
1 lb. Nestle Quik
$1/2$ lb. powdered sugar

$1/2$ lb. non-dairy creamer
$1/2$ tsp. salt

Mix and store in a cool, dry place. To serve, add 1 Tbsp. chocolate mix to 1 cup hot water, or to suit taste.

Hot Chocolate Mix

Sift 1 cup cocoa (or 2 lbs. Nestle Quik) and $1^1/2$ cups powdered sugar. Add 11 cups dry milk (IGA brand is best) and 6 oz. dry coffee cream substitute. Mix well. Store in covered container. To serve, put $1/3$ to $1/2$ cup dry mix in a cup, then fill up with hot water. Stir.

Café Bavarian Mint

$1/4$ cup coffee creamer
$1/4$ cup instant coffee
2 Tbsp. peppermint candy, broken

$1/3$ cup sugar
2 Tbsp. cocoa

Mix; use 1 Tbsp. of mix with 6 oz. boiling water.

Eggnog

4 eggs
$^1/_3$ cup sugar
$^1/_8$ tsp. nutmeg
4 tsp. lemon juice

$^1/_8$ tsp. salt
$^1/_2$ cup cream
4 cups milk

Beat eggs until thick; add sugar, nutmeg, lemon juice, and salt. Add ice cold cream and milk. Beat with eggbeater. You can omit lemon juice and add your preference.

Quick Root Beer

In a gallon jar, dissolve 1 tsp. yeast in 1 cup warm water. Add $1^1/_2$ cups sugar and 4 tsp. root beer extract and enough warm water to mix thoroughly until dissolved. Fill jar with water and set in a warm place, or sunlight, several hours, until strong enough; cool. Can be made in the morning and ready to drink by noon.

Iced Tea

Miss Mary Miller

3 oranges, sliced
3 lemons, sliced

4 cups white sugar
22 red rose tea bags

Put this in a 13 qt. mixing bowl. Pour 4 qts. boiling water on top. Let set till water is dark. Remove tea bags. Immediately pour ice in!

Popsicles

3 oz. Jell-O
1 env. Kool-Aid
1 cup sugar

2 cups cold water
2 cups hot water

Mix and freeze in Popsicle trays.

Grape or Blackberry Wine

1 gal. grapes or berries, mashed 1 gal. water

Let set 24 hours, then strain through a cloth. Add 3 lbs. white sugar to 1 gal. liquid. Skim off and stir every day. Let stand till done working, then bottle.

Wine

1 qt. red clover blossoms, with 1 orange, sliced
green leaves all off 1 gal. water
1 lemon, sliced 3 lb. sugar

Heat the last 4 ingredients to boiling point and pour over blossoms. Let set till lukewarm, then put 1 tsp. dry yeast in and stir every day. Let set till worked out mostly, then strain and put in jug. Put on cloth and corn cob tightly . This will let some fermenting out there yet, but cover crock tightly so those little sour flies won't get in.

Ritz Crackers   *Mrs. Emanuel R. Miller*

4 cups pastry flour 1 egg
$^1/_2$ cup brown sugar 1 tsp. baking powder
$^3/_4$ cup mixed butter and dash of salt
shortening

Mix like pie dough. Add 1 beaten egg and enough milk to wet. Roll thin and cut in squares. Sprinkle with salt. Bake at 350°.

Baking Powder   *Mrs. John (Sarah) Brenneman*

1 Tbsp. baking soda 2 Tbsp. cream of tartar
1 Tbsp. cornstarch

Fruit Dip

1¼ cups pineapple juice
⅓ cup white sugar
2 Tbsp. flour
1 egg yolk

1 Tbsp. butter
vanilla
salt

Cook this together. Stir while cooking.

3–4 oz. cream cheese   powdered sugar

Mix together. When mixture is room temperature, add 12 oz. Cool Whip.

Mexican Salad Dressing

Mrs. Melvin (Esther) Miller

1 cup sugar
¾ cup salad oil
5 Tbsp. Miracle Whip
2 tsp. prepared mustard
1 tsp. celery seed

¼ tsp. black pepper
¼ cup chopped onion
¼ cup vinegar
¼ cup water

Mix sugar and salad oil, then add Miracle Whip and rest of ingredients; mix well.

Vegetable Pizza

Crust:

2 cups flour
1 Tbsp. sugar
3 tsp. baking powder

1 tsp. salt
½ cup shortening
¾ cup milk

Filling:

16 oz. cream cheese
1½ c. mayonnaise or sour cream

1 pkg. Hidden Valley Ranch
   dressing mix

Crust: Bake at 425° for 10 minutes. Makes 1 cookie sheet.
Filling: Mix cream cheese, mayonnaise, and dressing mix. Spread over crust and top with vegetables (broccoli, cauliflower, onions, lettuce, peppers, tomatoes, carrots, radishes, and celery). Sprinkle grated cheese on top. Cut into squares.

Danish Dessert

$^1/_3$ cup white sugar
2 Tbsp. clear jell

$^1/_4$ cup strawberry Jell-O
2 cups water

Mix dry ingredients and water and bring to a boil. Different flavors of Jell-O can be used.

Pineapple Pecan Cheese Ball

16 oz. cream cheese, softened
8 oz. crushed pineapple, drained
$^1/_2$ cup chopped green pepper
$^1/_2$ cup chopped green onions

1 tsp. lemon pepper seasoning
1 tsp. seasoned salt
2 cups chopped pecans
assorted crackers

In a mixing bowl, whip cream cheese until smooth. Gently stir in pineapple, green pepper, onions, seasonings, and $^1/_2$ cup nuts. Turn out onto a sheet of plastic wrap and shape into a ball. Refrigerate several hours, or overnight. Before serving, roll cheese ball in remaining nuts. Serve with crackers. Yield: 12–14 servings.

Easy Vegetable Dip

8 oz. cream cheese
1 sm. onion, chopped fine

$^1/_2$ cup salad dressing

Mix all together. Serve with carrots, celery, cauliflower, radishes, peppers, broccoli, etc.

Peanut Butter Suet (for Birds)

1 cup lard (no substitute)
1 cup crunchy peanut butter
2 cups quick oats

2 cups cornmeal
1 cup flour
$^1/_3$ cup sugar

Melt lard and peanut butter and add rest of ingredients. May add other ingredients like sunflower seeds or raisins.

Christmas Aroma

1 stick cinnamon

2 tsp. whole cloves

1 cup water

peelings of 1 orange

Put all ingredients in a small saucepan. Bring to a boil and let simmer.
Makes your house smell real pleasant.

Plant Food

Mrs. Ammon (Lydia) Miller

When setting tomato plants, place 1 heaping Tbsp. Epsom salt in hole,
then set in plant. This keeps nematodes away and produces big tomatoes.

Silly Putty

In first bowl, mix well 2 cups Elmer's school glue and $1^1/2$ cups water. In
second bowl, dissolve 2 level tsp. of 20 Mule Team Borax in 1 cup warm
water. Add any food coloring desired. Slowly add and mix together the 2
bowls of ingredients. You may have to use your hands to mix thoroughly.
Store in tight container.

Play Dough

2 cups flour

$^1/2$ cup cornstarch

1 Tbsp. alum

2 cups water

1 cup salt

1 Tbsp. salad oil

Place all ingredients in a saucepan. Stir constantly over low heat until
mixture thickens into dough consistency. Remove from heat and let it cool
until it can be handled. Place on foil, waxed paper, or Formica top and
knead like bread dough until smooth. Add food coloring, if you wish.
Store in airtight container. Keeps for months.

wooden spoon wisdom

If you really want the last word of an
argument, try saying, "I guess you're right."

MISCELLANEOUS

Baby Wipes

2 cups boiling water
3 Tbsp. baby bath

1 Tbsp. baby oil

Cut 1 roll of Bounty towels in half. Remove center cardboard. Place upright in an airtight container and pour solution over it. Cover tightly and it's ready to use in 1 hour. The wipes can be pulled up from the center, just like store-bought ones, and torn off at any length.

Soap

Mrs. Aden (Sarah) Miller

2 boxes lye
3 qts. rain water
$9^1/_2$ lbs. lard or tallow (best mixed)

1 cup glycerine
4 Tbsp. Borax

Put lye and water together and let cool. Put everything together when grease is like honey.

Window Cleaner

$^1/_2$ cup ammonia, plain
$^1/_2$ cup water

$^1/_2$ cup alcohol

Mix together and use like Windex.

Window Cleaner

Mrs. Ammon (Lydia) Miller

Mix about 1 Tbsp. cornstarch in 1 qt. of water and soak a rag in solution. Wash your glass object, then dry off with clean cloth or newspaper. The glass will really sparkle and this cleaner won't leave streaks unless you put in too much cornstarch.

wooden spoon wisdom

Faults are like crooked buggy wheels...
we never notice our own, only those
of the buggy ahead of us.

INDEX

Soups

Pies

Cakes and Cookies

Desserts

Snacks and Candy

Miscellaneous